Disposable Dogs

Disposable Dogs

Heartwarming, True Stories of Courage and Compassion

Steve Swanbeck

ISBN: 0-615-88350-8
ISBN-13: 978-0-615-88350-2

Published by White Swan Publishing, 1 Green Hill Road, Chester, NJ 07930; 908-970-3072

Printed in the United States of America

Fourth printing 2009

Library of Congress Control Number: 2003114420

For all general information, contact: White Swan Publishing, 908-879-3072

Cover photo by Veronika Eberhardt Kocsor

Also by Steve Swanbeck:

Images of America: The Seeing Eye
Images of America: East Hanover

Contents

Introduction

Millions of dogs are abandoned and otherwise abused in the United States every year. Some of the lucky ones survive and go on to lead rewarding lives, thanks to compassionate, generous people who dedicate themselves to the well-being of animals. Shelters, rescue groups, sanctuaries and individuals with big hearts from around the country shared memorable "success stories" for this book.

Dogs and humans have kept each other company for an estimated 15,000 years. Sometimes the relationship is good and mutually beneficial; other times it is not. Despite their status as mankind's best friend, dogs are all too often considered disposable by countless individuals and by society as a whole.

As a result, every year at least two million dogs are needlessly put to death. Diligent spaying and neutering would cut this number significantly. Dogs of every breed, size, age and temperament desperately need homes. They are available for adoption at shelters and rescue groups across America.

Not everyone should adopt a pet, however. There's work involved, and expense. For many people, the reward is worth it. Those willing to put forth the effort are, more often than not, gifted with a grateful companion brimming with unconditional love.

This book is dedicated to
everyone who helps animals
in need.

Monk & Lady

It depends on what the definition of the word *growl* is, but by one account, Monk growled when he smelled marijuana. The five-year-old schipperke mix never inhaled, but he did growl. Maybe it was time for him to go.

The owners of the small, black dog with the curly tail and pointed ears surrendered him to Second Chance Animal Center in Shaftsbury, Vermont, on a lovely spring day. They said Monk was too "hyper." (Perhaps he should have inhaled.) Otherwise, he was a good dog—he loved to swim, ride in the car and could jump a six-foot-high fence with ease. There was no mention of whether or not he got the munchies, but on the surrender form the owners made it a point to list his pot-growling tendency.

Monk adjusted to shelter life fairly well. At first he was a bit wary of strangers, although that soon changed. "It took a little while for him to warm up, but once he did, he always wanted to stay next to you," explains Second Chance's Cynthia Meier. Schipperkes are known to be devoted and loyal. Cynthia describes Monk as "a real character" with a great personality and constant curiosity. He also looked a little like a bat.

1

Lady was another shelter guest who awaited adoption at the same time. She was a slightly timid German shepherd mix, brindle in color, and three or four years old. Owner allergies caused her surrender. "She was an all-around good dog," says Cynthia, obedient, gentle on the lead, and quick to obey a variety of commands. Indoors she acted rather sedate, but outdoors she shed her inhibitions and romped with the best of them. When Lady needed, or wanted, to go out, she patiently nudged Cynthia on the arm.

Second Chance staff members decided it would be worth a try to put Monk and Lady together; Monk's confidence might rub off. Although Lady was at first nervous about her new roommate, they soon developed a strong attachment. "We hoped they would be adopted together," says Cynthia. That happens, but not often.

As spring warmed to summer, the dogs waited for someone to come by who would offer them a good home. In July, David and Marian Lewis Wohlsen visited the shelter looking for a dog. They met Monk and liked him. The shy Lady stayed in the background as her good friend charmed his way into a new life. It looked as though she would remain behind.

Although Cynthia felt very happy for the little black dog, she believed it was necessary to let the couple know about the important bond between Monk and Lady. She told them how good they were together. Two dogs weren't part of the plan; nevertheless, David and Marian decided to say hello to the shepherd. When they approached, Lady immediately "went belly up," suggesting, *I'm the friendliest dog you'll ever meet. Please take me, too.*

Lady's reaction paid off. They all went home together. The adoption "turned out better than we ever could have imagined," David and Marian told Second Chance. The dogs share the house with two cats, and they get along great. One of Monk's favorite pastimes includes keeping close tabs on squirrels that hang around the bird feeders in the garden. His ancestors used to chase rats around barges, which could explain his fascination with backyard rodents. Lady joins in the fun when she feels the urge. From time to time, the family will stop by the shelter in their minivan, with Monk and Lady sitting in the back, happy, comfortable and secure. No growls. No allergies. Although they do get the munchies from time to time.

Brandy

Eighteen-month-old Adam Whalen fiddled with his toys on the front porch while his mother, Sara, went inside the house to fix him lunch. It was a picturesque autumn afternoon in upstate New York, the trees awash with red, orange and gold leaves in their final stages of brilliance. When she walked back outside a few minutes later, fear pounced on the young mother, and her life changed forever. "Adam was gone," she remembers. "The toys were still there, but not Adam."

Sara frantically combed their property and the surrounding area looking for her toddler. She knocked on neighbors' doors to ask for help, but few were home. Local police arrived and searched for three hours without success. They called state troopers who flew in helicopters to obtain a bird's-eye view. Sara's husband rushed home from work. "I was hysterical," says Sara. "We could not find Adam. We didn't know if he'd been abducted. We didn't know if he was alive. We could not find him."

Six hours into the search a neighbor asked about Brandy, the 11-year-old golden retriever who lived next door to Sara and occasionally visited Adam. Perhaps the dog and the child were together. One of the state troopers remembered hearing a dog barking in the distance during an earlier foot search. Everyone started yelling for Brandy, and soon they heard a faint response. The search party ran toward the barking, following the sound deeper and deeper into the woods, until they came upon a sight that will remain etched in their memories forever.

There was Adam, "standing up, fast asleep, pressed against the trunk of a tree," explains Sara. "Brandy was holding him there with one shoulder. One of her legs was hanging over a thirty-five-foot drop to a stream below. It was perfectly obvious that she saved his life. She must have followed Adam when he wandered off, just as a dog will with a child, and she saw danger. She pushed him out of harm's way and held him there. This was an old dog. Adam was an 18-month-old child. He struggled, I'm sure, but she held him there for all those hours. When I picked him up, she collapsed." As a trooper carried the scratched but otherwise uninjured boy back to his house, Sara, sobbing with relief, hoisted Brandy into her arms and carried the weary dog back, too. The moment marked a turning point in Sara's life and a new beginning for Brandy.

Sara grew up in a pets non grata household. They were considered dirty and unwanted. "Animals were not part of my experience, so I had no conscience about them," she says. Sara basically ignored animals even after her family moved next door to Brandy and her owner, an elderly woman who tended a garden with the cheerful, tail-wagging Brandy lying by her side. Shortly before the life-saving episode, the old woman died. Her relatives showed up afterward, cleaned out the house and put it up for sale. With the deceased woman undoubtedly turning over in her grave, they locked Brandy out and drove away. The dog had no idea what to do. She hung around the house during the day and slept on the porch at night. A neighbor fed her, but that was the extent of her care. At that point, it didn't cross Sara's mind to worry about the abandoned dog with the dark golden coat and lonesome gray face.

Sara's appreciation for animals changed the moment she realized Brandy saved her child's life. "From then on, I made it a point to learn everything I could about animals," she says. Sara started rescuing old golden retrievers and eventually founded Pets Alive, an animal sanctuary in Middletown, New York. On any given day, there are hundreds of animals living at the facility, including dogs, cats, chickens, goats, pot-bellied pigs, birds and retired New York City carriage horses. Brandy, who moved in permanently with the Whalens, inspired the whole thing. "Because of Brandy, thousands of unwanted animals have been given safe lives," says Sara. Not a bad legacy for a friendly old golden whose tail never stopped wagging.

Missy

The gray toy poodle woke up one morning and realized she was all alone in the world. She wasn't quite sure how or why it happened, but that didn't matter much anymore. Finding a scrap to eat and a safe place to rest became the cute little dog's primary interests, until she bumped into a handsome young terrier who charmed his way into her heart and introduced her to motherhood. In no time at all, she had three other mouths to feed, her boyfriend was long gone, and the outdoor temperature in Rome, Georgia, dropped as winter approached. She needed to find a safe haven . . . soon.

When the puppies were old enough to walk a distance, they followed closely as mom tramped through grass and woods near a busy roadway, searching for food and water, while several of nature's more irritating parasites embedded themselves in the easy prey. Hunger became an obsession for the mother and children, as her milk dried up and they trudged on. Just when hope started to fade, the poodle spotted something; she saw the corpse of a deer lying on the ground. It had probably been hit by a car, stumbled as far away from the road as its legs would carry, took one final breath and then fell over dead. The deer's misfortune could turn out to be the dogs' salvation.

Mom sniffed the carcass up and down before taking a few bites and offering tiny bits of nourishment to her starving youngsters. It wasn't exactly kibble, but fetid venison would keep them alive for another day. After enough of the deer was gnawed away, the mother came up with another idea: use the remains as a shelter to protect the puppies from the elements when she took off briefly to search for answers on what to do next.

One day she got lucky. A volunteer with the Rome-Floyd County Humane Society discovered the poodle walking along by herself. When the woman approached, the dog begged her to follow and headed straight for the puppies who were resting inside the deer carcass. The woman had never seen anything like it before but, no matter, the dogs were alive and needed help. "I don't think they would have lasted many more days," says Ann Turner, who operates a foster home for the society. Ann agreed to take the dogs when the woman who rescued them brought the malnourished family to the humane society.

The next stop for the dogs was the veterinarian, who treated them for mange, worms and ear mites. "We got them nice and healthy and then put them up for adoption," explains Ann. The puppies were easy to place. One relocated to the State of Washington with a local family who had just moved west. A young couple from Rome adopted another, and the third went home with a woman who was recently widowed. Mom, who was named Missy, was adopted by a woman enjoying her golden years. She loved the dog and doted on Missy like an unbridled grandmother. They strolled around town together, rode in the car, watched TV, and never seemed to be apart. Missy owned every imaginable pet toy and dined on chicken nightly. They truly enjoyed each other's company until, sadly, a few years after they met, the woman died.

Ann once again took in Missy, this time permanently. "I decided I would not put her through any more changes and that she would stay with me the rest of her life," says Ann. Missy still loves to ride in the car and is especially happy when they stop at the bank, where the tellers are quick to offer snacks. She shares Ann's home with five other permanent dogs plus six to ten fosters, depending on how busy things get. At night, she sleeps in Ann's bed with three dachshunds. "She loves it here," says Ann. "She's a very happy dog."

When foster puppies are in the house, Missy assumes the role of mother. "She likes to think of them as her own," says Ann. Once a month Missy visits her biological daughter, Muffin, who lives close by. In addition to the traditional nudging and tail wagging, they reminisce in a doggy sort of way. They're understandably grateful that the hard times are over. And if they never again taste venison, that will be just fine by them.

Capone

As he cut the chain and the dead dog blinked, Scotlund Haisely thought to himself: "Now I have an emergency on my hands."

It was a hot, humid summer day in the nation's capital when a woman telephoned the humane society to report she had been looking out the window of her row house and watching a dog starve to death in a neighbor's yard. Well, it finally died, she thought, and it smelled, and she wanted the carcass removed. "I responded to the call," says Scotlund, who pulled up to the rundown house, looked over a chain-link fence into the trash-strewn backyard and saw a black-and-tan dog lying motionless in overgrown grass. It was attached to a chain, emaciated and covered with flies. There was no food, water, doghouse or any other form of shelter. Algae flourished in a nearby empty bowl.

With enough evidence to enter the property, the Washington Humane Society officer jumped over the fence and approached the dog, who definitely appeared dead. It was another unfortunate, routine assignment. He would confiscate the dog's body to be used to mount a case for an animal cruelty prosecution. "I cut the chain with my bolt cutters," explains Scotlund, and, much to his surprise, the dog blinked. He touched the weak, frightened animal and there was some slight movement. It needed medical attention, quickly.

Scotlund shooed away a group of flies, picked up the thin, young rottweiler and started walking toward his van. Suddenly, he heard the angry voice of a man cursing in his direction. The officer kept going; he hopped a fence, hurried to his vehicle and locked the animal inside. "I didn't want him to get the dog back in his hands," explains Scotlund. With the dog safe, it was time to have a chat with the owner. After they met face to face and the owner became verbally aggressive, Scotlund called for assistance.

By the time police arrived, the owner admitted he neglected his pet, claiming he couldn't afford to take care of it. In inner cities throughout the country, people often get rottweilers or pit bulls for their own protection and then sometimes fail to protect the dogs. The man's story didn't convince the police, who arrested him for animal cruelty. (A judge later sentenced him to three years probation and forbid him from owning another dog for three years.)

Scotlund rushed the dog to a veterinary hospital where the doctor determined it had only hours to live. They decided to try to save it. Scotlund visited the dog the next day because, he admits: "There was something about him that drew me to him. His eyes were innocent and confused. There was an immediate bond, although I could say that about all the dogs I've rescued over the years." It took several weeks, but good health returned; the dog's will to live overpowered the damage inflicted by his environment. During that time, Scotlund decided to adopt the friendly patient and named him Capone.

"He's been my inspiration ever since," Scotlund says. "He's never left my side." Capone quickly learned the basics of obedience, so Scotlund decided to take his gentle pet along when he gave humane education talks at inner-city schools. "He's the ideal dog because he's a rottweiler," says Scotlund. "It's important for kids in the inner cities to see dogs responding to compassion."

During their career together, the pair have worked in Washington, New York City, San Francisco, and then back in DC, where Scotlund now serves as executive director of the Washington Animal Rescue League. Thanks to the affectionate dog who nearly starved to death at the end of a chain, countless children have learned how to better care for their own pets.

❧

Wolf

If it looks like a wolf, paces back and forth like a wolf, and prefers steak tartar over a well-done T-bone, it's probably a wolf. This one is, regardless of the story told upon his surrender to the Berkley County Humane Society in Martinsburg, West Virginia.

One day a man came to the shelter with a large gray animal wearing a thick, six-foot chain around its neck. The man said it was a shepherd-husky mix he spotted wandering around. When he stopped his car, the animal jumped in, so he took it home and locked it in a room. He said he left the house to pick up his two-year-old daughter and, upon his return, found the room destroyed. Nonetheless, he let his daughter play with the creature, but things got a little too rough, so the man decided to bring it to the humane society. (People who run shelters hear all kinds of tales and generally don't challenge their authenticity. They accept the unwanted animals and do the best they can.)

"When he first came in, you could tell that his logging chain was his life," says the humane society's Donna Holmes. "He obviously had been tied in a backyard to his chain." It was also clear that this pup was no dog. A year and a half earlier, the shelter rescued a wolf that they managed to place in a petting zoo in Virginia. The similarities were undeniable.

They named the young wolf, Wolf, and began researching rescue organizations that specialize in the species. He was friendly and not at all aggressive, so the staff played with him every day. Wolves often get a bad rap thanks, in part, to misguided nursery rhymes.

"He grew to love all of us very much," says Donna. He especially liked playing tug-of-war with freshly cleaned laundry as his new friends tried to fold it up and put it away. Wolf's favorite toy was a stuffed clown that he would take from its storage container, play with, then put it back in the container when he was through. "He did better than most kids," Donna admits. "Wolf was very, very, very intelligent."

As much as Wolf enjoyed his temporary digs and all the kind attention, he still yearned for a more spacious environment with members of his own breed. The heart of a wild animal beat in Wolf's chest as he paced back and forth, back and forth in the kennel. One day while he was in a run next to a litter of small puppies, one of them stuck its little paw through an opening and into Wolf's pen. As the staff watched Wolf walk toward it, and before they could do anything, the consensus was, "oh, no, we're soon going to have a three-legged puppy." That, however, wasn't Wolf's nature. He leaned his head down and gently nudged the puppy's paw back inside its own pen where it belonged.

That's not to say that Wolf didn't like to eat. The first few days at the shelter, he ate dog food and came down with a nasty case of diarrhea. Donna consulted an expert who said to feed him raw hunks of chicken. It turned out that he actually liked his chicken lightly broiled but did enjoy a raw steak or chuck roast. On one occasion, he ate an entire ham, bone and all. "We kept spoiling him," admits Donna, "feeding him and spoiling him."

Wolf quickly became a local celebrity. People came to the shelter to bring him food, pet him if they dared, or have their picture taken together. "He really got to be popular," says Donna.

Then about a month after he arrived, the humane society found a more appropriate home—a wolf sanctuary in Tennessee that would treat him well. Parting was bittersweet. Everyone knew Wolf would be better off living in a place more suited to his lifestyle. On the other hand, they had grown very fond of him. "He was special," says Donna. She remembers vividly that when the driver came to pick up Wolf and they hoisted him into the truck "we cried like babies."

By now the tears have dried and Wolf is "doing wonderfully." He's safe, well fed, and has lots of his own property to roam around. He also has a special friend: a female wolf with whom he shares his accommodations. She's spayed, so there won't be any little wolves in the future, but it is nice to have someone to share life's little pleasures . . . like an entire ham, bone and all.

Aussie

Janet Hartman pushed herself hard that summer. There were so many things to do. The Rhode Island real estate market kept her very busy, plus there were all those details associated with her son's upcoming wedding. After awhile, she started feeling run down, then lousy, and eventually wound up in bed taking antibiotics. They didn't work, but the doctor said Janet would be fine. The prognosis proved incorrect.

One day as Janet rested in bed and her husband Robert "Hoot" napped in another room, something went dreadfully wrong. Her electrolytes crashed, her brain filled with fluid and she went into convulsions. As the unconscious Janet shook violently and gasped for breath, her constant companion, Aussie, sprang to her feet, recognized there was a crisis, and dashed off to awaken Hoot. The Australian cattle dog-greyhound mix alerted him, and he hurried to his wife's side.

Realizing the situation was serious, Hoot called 911, and the rescue squad arrived just in time. Janet was rushed to the hospital where she remained in intensive care for ten days. "I would have died in bed, without a doubt, had she not gone to get my husband," says Janet. Both Janet and Hoot missed the wedding, but she was alive and recovering.

When Janet first met the blue-merle colored dog at the Providence Animal Rescue League, she didn't look much like a heroine. In fact, Aussie acted aloof. "She must have been disgusted with her lot in life," remembers Janet. Aussie first turned up at the shelter when she was two months old, but her original owner claimed her. Nine months later, he returned her to the shelter. It seems the dog's energy level was too high to suit him and, besides, he really didn't have time for her. Abandoned and confined, Aussie grew depressed.

So why did Janet select a dog seemingly disinterested in the prospect of adoption? She had never seen a dog that looked like her before, or one with such an attitude. In addition, they called her Australia, and Janet's son was interested in traveling to Australia. "What are the odds?" Janet asks. She thought about it for a time and decided this was the dog to take home.

When she's not performing heroic deeds or driving around with Janet keeping an eye on real estate prices, Aussie plays with the Hartman's chocolate lab, Cocoa, who was also adopted from the Providence Animal Rescue League. They get along like sisters. In addition to her natural instinct to "run like the wind," herd everyone and everything in sight, and keep tabs on the entire family, Aussie has an affinity for those perfume samples that come in direct mail advertisements. Smart, friendly and fragrant! Now that's a dog worth keeping, high energy level or not.

"I tell her all the time how special she is," says Janet, special enough that Hoot decided an official recognition was in order. One morning the retired military man summoned Janet, Aussie and Cocoa into the living room and presented the cattle dog with a Good Conduct Medal he, himself, earned in the service. He thanked Aussie for saving his wife's life and then concluded the ceremony with a heartfelt salute to the heroine. She wears the medal on her collar to this day.

Keeley

No one knows for sure how long the old dog sprawled motionless along the river bank. She had been shot, bludgeoned and left for dead, except the person who tried to kill her failed to complete the task.

One crisp autumn day a fisherman found her, barely alive, and called authorities, expecting the poor thing to be picked up and put out of her misery. When he went fishing the next day, to his surprise, the dog was still lying there, alive. He contacted the authorities again. Perhaps the fish were biting, maybe it was his curiosity, but the sportsman returned to the same spot the following day. Amazingly, there she was, all alone, clinging to life. He went home and contacted different people.

At around ten p.m., Ava Bothe Swartslander received a call from her veterinarian who explained the situation. Ava is the founder of Animal Lifeline of Iowa in Carlisle, and her shelter is located only a few miles from the river. As she received directions on where to find the bloodied and battered victim, thunder rumbled in the distance; it sounded like it was headed their way. Ava and a volunteer decided to search for the dog immediately. If alive, it probably wouldn't last through a stormy night.

Animal Lifeline is a no-kill special needs shelter that accepts homeless dogs and cats who are sick, injured, pregnant, nursing, orphaned or handicapped. "We try to take in animals that are least likely to make it," Ava explains.

Guided by flashlights, she and her companion searched slowly and carefully along the riverbank in the pitch darkness. It took five to ten minutes to find the immobile animal who was partially covered with leaves and brush. Ava bent down and tried to detect a pulse. She found one, so they lifted the fifty-pound mutt onto a stretcher, carried her up the embankment, placed her gently in the car and headed straight for the vet.

Upon examination, the veterinarian found the nine- or ten-year-old had been shot in the right front leg and beaten over the head. It seems the shooter was a lousy marksman, so he clobbered her with a blunt instrument to try to kill her. Evidently, this wasn't the dog's first taste of abuse. The vet discovered "terrible" ear infections and practically no hair on her body, the result of untreated allergies and a malfunctioning thyroid. As the dog drifted in and out of consciousness, Ava stared down at her and thought that "she was the most pathetic looking thing I've ever seen in my life." They decided to let the dog rest through the night and see what the morning would bring. It didn't look promising.

But this was one tenacious dog. She awoke the next day alert and ready to continue her struggle to survive. "I think this old lady wants to live," Ava said to the doctor. "Let's go for it." Unfortunately, the leg was too far gone to save, but the rest of her was repairable. After months of treatment and loving care, the dog recuperated. Her hair grew back and it was blonde. Ava named her Keeley, an Irish Gaelic word that means beautiful. "After all she went through, I figured she deserved it."

Even after losing a front leg at an advanced age, Keeley didn't slow down. She remained at Animal Lifeline for the rest of her days and had a rich and rewarding time. She had the run of the facility, playing with people and animals every day, including another dog who had been shot and survived.

"Keeley thoroughly enjoyed her life," says Ava. "She always had the will to live." Humans could take a lesson from dogs who have suffered but refused to give up. "They never look back. They just pick up and go forward."

❦

Dakota

When the husband and wife divorced, neither wanted to take their pet—a big, playful Saint Bernard who wasn't yet two years old. He was a handsome specimen, white with reddish-brown markings and a mask over each eye. Although very friendly, he was no saint; now and then he discovered that mischief had its merits. By any standard, he was a great dog, but his owners surrendered Dakota to the Louisiana SPCA nonetheless.

Shelter workers enjoyed playing with the purebred and seeing to his basic needs, but their deepest hope was that someone with a good home would soon adopt him. Dakota, of course, had no idea what was going on. One day he was a family pet, then all of a sudden he sat in a kennel surrounded by strangers. Days and nights passed slowly, as did Dakota's chances for adoption. The SPCA hated the thought of euthanizing the healthy, young dog; however, this is the sad reality faced by shelters throughout the country that overflow with unwanted animals.

Much to everyone's sorrow, Dakota finally reached the end of the road; at least he could see it from his kennel. There might, however, be one last chance. A call was placed to Marie and Joseph Marcal. The Marcals previously adopted an Akita from the LA/SPCA; perhaps the family would consider taking a second dog. As they drove to the shelter, the Marcals understood full well that if they met Dakota—petted him, looked deeply into his sad eyes—the reprieve would be assured. "We took him right home," says Marie. "I can't believe his parents gave him away . . . their loss."

Dakota settled comfortably into the big, old house in New Orleans. "He loved everybody from the get-go," says Marie. Not shy about stealing shoes, opening up the garbage can to see if there was anything interesting inside, or wolfing down an entire batch of freshly made pralines, Dakota brought additional spunk to the household. "He's just a big baby, a 200-pound two-year-old."

At the same time Dakota adjusted to his new lifestyle, the New Orleans Saints decided to reinstate an animal as the professional football team's dog mascot. The SPCA suggested that Dakota be interviewed for the prestigious position. Freshly bathed and placed on his best behavior, Dakota tackled the challenge with poise and enthusiasm. He got the job and soon found himself greeting adoring fans at the Superdome before each home game. "He's the friendliest thing in the world," says a Saints spokesman. "The people seem to really like him."

His amiable disposition landed Dakota weekday employment as well. "The Big Giant Head," as he's affectionately referred to on occasion, is the receptionist at Joseph's law firm. He keeps the "Dakota drool" to a minimum while on the clock.

With things getting a little too quiet around the house, the Marcals subsequently adopted two more dogs, mother and son Louisiana catahoula leopards. Once a week, all four dogs visit the veterinarian for a bath. Dakota is too big to fit in the tub, so they hose him down outside. From unwanted sinner to immaculate saint, The Big Giant Head did all right for himself.

cᴎᴎᴎᴑ

Aggie

The grandmother lived quietly in a modest house with her faithful dog, an old husky mix named Aggie. They loved each other dearly and spent most of the time just taking it easy as the sun rose and set over their small Michigan town. The pair had been together for years, ever since Barbara saved Aggie from an abusive environment. But that unfortunate episode was long forgotten. Life turned out well—peaceful and predictable.

Then one day Barbara disappeared. Aggie didn't know what to do. She missed her companion desperately and had to find her. Determined and focused, the dog took off and started looking. The search led to the local hospital. Thanks to an electronic door, Aggie let herself in. Hospital employees threw her out. She tried again. Once more, they escorted her from the facility. Aggie knew Barbara was in there. She was right, but how she figured it out is one of those animal enigmas that fascinates anyone who gives it even the slightest consideration. Aggie tried one more time. Three attempts and she was out for good. Authorities arrived and hauled the lonely old dog off to the pound.

She wore no identification tag, and no one claimed her. Barbara didn't know her loyal pet sat in a cage, depressed and only hours away from the dreamless sleep. On the morning Aggie was scheduled to die, Fran Sinnott and Rose Casperson of Lakeshore Animal Friends in Ludington intervened. Their group rescues animals whose time runs out at the pound. By then, though, it really didn't seem to matter to Aggie. "It was like she had no hope," says Fran. "She had no enthusiasm for life."

Fran resolved to change that. She brought Aggie to live in her own house until an adoptive family could be found. Despite Fran's efforts, the dog never fully snapped out of her funk. "She seemed to appreciate her new environment but still appeared to be ill at ease and depressed," explains Fran. When the rescuer took the dog for walks to try to cheer her up, Aggie always stared toward the southwest as if something beckoned. The dog missed Barbara and her own home, but Fran had no way of knowing. "I mistook Aggie's depression to be the result of possible abuse," she admits.

A few weeks later, on Thanksgiving morning, Fran decided to take Aggie with her when she went out. Aggie was off the leash as they walked down the driveway to get in the truck. Instead of stopping next to the vehicle, however, Aggie kept walking. Fran called to her. Aggie turned and looked at Fran with grateful, determined eyes as if to say *thanks for everything, but I have to do this*, and then turned and hurried away.

"She was on a mission," says Fran, who jumped in the truck to try to catch her. The dog proved elusive, moving faster and faster along the streets and across intersections. The chase lasted less than a mile, when Aggie deliberately turned down a lane. As Fran caught up with her, a boy grabbed the dog by the collar. Fran told him to let go. He refused. "This is my grandma's dog," he told her.

Amid the excitement, Barbara ran out of a nearby house barefoot, in her nightgown, and sat down on the stoop. The dog bounded to her side, they embraced in a tearful reunion, and Aggie's depression drifted away in the autumn wind along with the aroma of roasting turkeys.

లు

Portugal & Lisbon

A bright sun rose over the mountain, and the sweet scent of Mediterranean flora drifted lazily in the clear morning air following a violent storm that thundered through the small village of Malveira da Serra the night before. Lynne and Steve prepared for another uncharted day as American expatriates living on the western shore of Portugal. Lynne served as general manager of a major pharmaceutical company; Steve was basically along for the ride, together with their two Bernese mountain dogs and a neighbor's cat who decided the warm Portuguese climate would be easier on his aging joints than New Jersey winters.

"I hear someone at the front door," Lynne told her husband as she headed in that direction. She opened the door to find a darling surprise that would endear and complicate their lives for the next several months.

Snuggled together atop the doormat, looking very much like characters in a Disney movie, were two bedraggled dogs who had escaped the pouring rain beneath an overhanging roof. Lynne and Steve immediately recognized the young orphans; they had been lounging on the street in front of their house the day before—a dangerous pastime on the serpentine, highly traveled mountain road.

The expatriates loved animals and had saved several abandoned dogs before, but it was a difficult undertaking in Portugal. Strays roamed through most towns and cities, much more so than the Americans were used to back home. They knew of only one shelter, and it left a lot to be desired. The question was: "What do we do with these two?"

They were cute, frightened and alone in the world. The dogs were obviously unrelated. The senior of the pair appeared to be about a year old. She was a sweet-tempered, light-brown mixed breed who looked as if she might have some Irish setter in her bloodline. Her female companion, also a mutt, was a puppy, mostly black with a bit of white here and there, and tight fur similar to a Portuguese water dog. They were adorable, lying there together and looking up with forlorn eyes wondering what these two foreigners were about to do next. No one had a clue.

They couldn't put the dogs back on the street. They couldn't keep them either; two pampered Berners and a curmudgeonly cat wouldn't stand for it. Lynne and Steve tried to find a home for the dogs in Portugal, but there were no takers. They asked people back home, but again no one was interested. Just as desperation started setting in, Steve got a call saying that his uncle and aunt, Bill and Jeanne Wright, and their son, Jon, would each take a dog. There was relief in Malveira da Serra that afternoon.

Not many strays have the opportunity to travel outside their neighborhoods, but these two were about to take a transatlantic flight in the belly of a jumbo jet. The flight from Lisbon to Newark was uneventful (at least Lynne and Steve perceived it that way). When the two families and two dogs met for the first time at Bill and Jeanne's home in Caldwell, New Jersey, the affection was contagious. Bill and Jeanne latched on to the black-and-white puppy and named her Lisbon. Jon, his wife, Libby, and their three children selected the one-year-old and named her Portugal. The two lucky strays had come a long way, but there were still a few surprises ahead.

Not long after they settled into a comfortable life as two of America's newest immigrants, Portugal started acting a bit peculiar. One night while she was staying with Bill and Jeanne, she went into labor. The vet had earlier confirmed that this was coming, so Bill had constructed a whelping box and put it in a bedroom. By six the next morning, with a lot of help from Bill, six healthy puppies had joined the family.

There was more doggie adoption work to be done. Jon and family were up to the task, however; within a few months they found new homes for all six puppies. Meanwhile, Lisbon, a puppy of considerable enthusiasm and intelligence, brought an unmatched joy to Bill and Jeanne. "That mutt, every morning she amazes me," Bill says. "She's absolutely perfect."

Portugal and family have since moved to upstate New York, near Syracuse, where Jon occasionally indulges in thespian pursuits. In a theatre production of *Annie,* he landed the part of Franklin Delano Roosevelt, while the role of Sandy, Annie's beloved dog, went to Portugal.

Years after the thunderstorm in the mountains, the two orphans from across the sea now go to bed each night knowing full well that, for them, the sun'll come out tomorrow.

Howie

Howie scooped up the tennis ball and returned it to the sick little girl. She tossed it again, and Howie repeated the exercise. After a few more throws, it was her sister's turn and then her brother's. This was a wish come true for the three siblings who suffered from a terrible, debilitating disease. Although the ball never traveled more than a few feet with each exhausting fling, the friendly black dog fetched it time and again that afternoon in the yard at the Helen Woodward Animal Center in Rancho Santa Fe, California.

The youngsters arrived at the animal center courtesy of the Make-A-Wish Foundation. They were from the Midwest and longed for the chance to visit Sea World and a working animal shelter. The kids had a ball with Howie and hugged and kissed him with a healthy dose of childish affection when it was time to go. Witnessing the children's joy provided their parents a moment of happiness as well.

Howie practices good deeds on a regular basis, but only because someone did right by him just in the nick of time. He had been a stray living on the streets of San Diego, scrounging for food and dodging traffic in an effort to survive. He was picked up on a December day by

31

animal control officers and ended up at a holiday pet adoption event at the San Diego County Fairgrounds. For the skinny black mutt with the name Bones on his kennel, this was his last chance. When it comes to adoption, black dogs don't fare as well as lighter colored dogs. Odds were the street dog with protruding ribs probably wouldn't live to see too many more sunsets over the Pacific.

Then John Van Zante, public relations manager at the Helen Woodward Animal Center, came along. John was at the fairgrounds looking for a new dog, just the right companion. When he first saw Bones, John thought: "he was the wrong size, the wrong breed, too skinny and too nervous. But this was the one that put his paw on my leg, told me he had been waiting, and now it was time for me to take him home. Later that afternoon, Bones became Howie and we started life together. He was perfect"

Out of curiosity, John asked the adoption processor how much longer they would have kept Bones. The answer: "You just saved his life."

One of the first objectives when they got home was to put some meat on Howie's bones. "Those first couple of months, he could not eat enough," explains John. "After scouting the house to make sure he wasn't going to have to fight another dog for the food, he would take a bite of food, walk two steps, and drop it on the floor. Then another bite was dropped behind the dining room table. Others went in the master bedroom and the downstairs hallway. Once he had made his stashes, he would eat the food in his bowl and lick it clean. After the bowl was empty, he would go back to eat the piles. It took a few months before he trusted that he was going to be fed and that no other dog was going to take away his food if he didn't hide it."

Now well fed and secure in a loving home, Howie goes to the animal shelter every day with John and works with people and other animals. He helps puppies who arrive at the center without a mother to understand puppy protocol, the social graces expected of young dogs. "He's big enough that the puppies will respect his growl, but gentle enough that he would never hurt a puppy that tries to steal his rawhide chew or invade his food bowl," explains John.

Howie often participates in the animal center's Dog Smart program that helps people overcome their canine fears. One case involved three boys who walked to school and were constantly late for class because they strayed far off course to avoid all the neighborhood dogs. Howie worked with them to allay their anxieties.

He's also spent time with autistic children. John remembers that one child "walked right up to Howie, cupped both hands and reached out to cradle Howie's tail. For him, the fact that there was a dog attached to the tail was totally inconsequential. He just stood there and stared at the long, furry thing in his hands. When I spoke Howie's name, he began to wag. The little boy's face broke into a huge grin and he squealed with laughter."

꩜

Stormy

Stormy paced back and forth in the snow next to the beat-up old car that secured him like a convict's ball to his chain. Occasionally he curled up on the hood to protect himself from the cold or to watch the other manacled dogs, some dead, others nearly so. The husky-malamute mix with eyes of blue and a thick gray-and-white coat saw a nearby dilapidated bus, listened to anguished barking coming from inside and smelled foul odors that wafted through the chilled air. He was strong; that's why he survived this long, but Stormy couldn't last forever.

Then one day in November, help arrived. Television viewers watched in horror as Alaska's Society for the Prevention of Cruelty to Animals exposed the grim evidence of scores of dogs hoarded under despicable conditions by an alleged breeder in the town of Sterling. Some were crammed into crates and stuffed inside the rusting bus, including an Australian border collie and her five puppies who endured in a small box with no light or heat and scarcely any food. Others froze or starved to death while chained outdoors. Their carcasses hardened in the snow.

"Here is the proof that Alaska needs an enforcement officer to put some muscle in the anticruelty laws that are in place and to encourage responsible stewardship from those that choose to make their fortune from the flesh of living beings," says the SPCA.

The dogs, purebreds and mutts, were hungry, thirsty and in need of medical attention. Infection swelled Stormy's ear, and an old injury flared up in his back. Nonetheless, he was overjoyed to see the cavalry arrive. "Despite his obvious suffering, he playfully extended his paw to his rescuers," explains Holly Okon of the SPCA. "As with the other dogs that were rescued, Stormy is a true testament of a dog's will to live. Despite neglect and human indifference, he remained trusting of people."

Stormy and sixty-five other dogs made it out alive and were transported to Anchorage. There, the SPCA fed the starving animals, provided medical care, bathed, groomed and exercised them, and put the revitalized dogs up for adoption. With all the media attention, most of them found new homes quickly.

"By the end of the winter, all of the dogs had been placed, except for one: Stormy. He was the sweetest boy," says Holly. "You felt special when you walked that dog. Though he enjoyed the attention of shelter workers and volunteers, he craved human affection, and it was obvious he needed a family of his own."

Even as the calendar advanced to summer, Stormy remained at the shelter. One day a woman walked in looking for a big dog and was introduced to the handsome, ninety-pound Sterling survivor. "She was immediately smitten with Stormy," says Holly. After a few tail wags and hugs, Stormy said goodbye to those who saved his life and headed home with his new companion, a television news woman who reported on the story. According to the latest reports, Stormy is a happy, pampered "ladies man" who now spends most of his time indoors, undoubtedly watching TV.

❧

Buck

Lightning flashed across the rural Tennessee sky as a fierce summer storm dumped buckets of rain on the sheriff deputy's car while he drove to the caller's home. It was nighttime, and the officer dreaded what he was about to do.

Earlier a family phoned the sheriff's office because a dog had been hanging around their house creating a nuisance. They wanted the authorities to come out and shoot it—not unheard of in those parts. For the deputy, this presented a dilemma; he loved dogs. Although he was doing his job, it was a difficult moment for the officer when he arrived at his destination and opened the car door. As he slowly walked toward the house, out of nowhere a young, soaking-wet black Labrador mix leapt into the police car, plopped down on the front seat, and began eating the deputy's lunch. Labs waste little time worrying about inhibitions.

Unsure of his next move and not about to start blasting holes in the interior of the car, the deputy climbed in and drove off. As the lab made himself comfortable and polished off a bag of potato chips, the officer placed a call to see if there was anything he could

37

do for this friendly puppy who was so full of life. He surely didn't want to kill it.

There was no animal control facility in the area, but there might be an opportunity at Home at Last, a small animal sanctuary run by Lee and David Hoover in Centerville. The Hoovers are animal lovers who are devoted to rescuing abandoned and abused animals and giving them a loving home. At times, they have taken in as many as ninety dogs and cats at their five-acre homestead. They do all the work—that's a lot of work—and pay all the bills themselves. When they find very good homes for their pets, they adopt them out. Otherwise, the animals remain at Home at Last for the rest of their lives.

"The deputy just didn't want to kill him and didn't know what to do," Lee recalls. So the police dispatcher got in touch with Lee. Naturally, she told him to bring the dog over.

In the pouring rain, Lee and the deputy ushered the animal into a four-foot-high, chain-link run and then turned to go inside. No sooner had they taken a step when the frisky puppy hopped the fence, made a beeline for the police car, and jumped in once again. "He was ready for another ride," Lee remembers. "He was a typical, friendly, six-month-old, gangly puppy."

Buck, as the dog was later named, was then escorted to a six-foot-high run. Lee offered Buck some food and water and went to bed. "The next morning, when I opened my door, he was sitting on my front porch," says Lee. That day they took Buck to the vet because, despite his enthusiasm, he had a nasty injury. Not long before the rainy night, Buck had either been hit over the head or shot at an angle; there was a groove caked with dried blood along the top of his head. How this happened is anyone's guess.

Several years later, Buck is doing just fine. He plays with the other dogs and finally grew tired of hopping the fence. Lee and David provide lots of love and attention. "He's just a clown," says Lee. "Of course, labs are." This lab, once homeless and closer to death than he'll ever know, is home at last.

❦

Ralph & Samantha

They took walks together, rode in the car together, even enjoyed a weekly massage together. The blind old lady and deaf, wobbly legged old man were nearly inseparable. At the tail end of their long and often lonely lives, they found one another.

"I took so much pleasure watching them enjoying each other's company," explains Deborah Workman, founder of The Sanctuary for Senior Dogs in Cleveland, Ohio. "They were soul mates . . . never far from each other, often sitting together just passing the time, sharing a patch of sunshine and holding paws."

Life wasn't always that cozy for either of the dogs, although Samantha had a much better go of it than Ralph. Samantha was eleven when Deborah adopted her from a no-kill animal sanctuary. She lived most of her life there and had recently been blinded in a fire. Although the reddish-brown retriever mix received excellent care and attention, Deborah felt that Samantha would do better in a home setting, so she opened up her own home.

It's hard to imagine what initially went through Samantha's mind. Her limited world centered around the comfort of her sanctuary until one day she awoke from a terrible nightmare and could no longer see. Soon thereafter she was riding in a car unable to enjoy the passing vistas, flying on an airplane and then entering a strange house that was already home to unfamiliar dogs and cats. Despite the lifestyle change, "she fit in almost immediately," Deborah remembers.

Ralph spent much of his ten years chained to a truck at a garden center, with little to eat. He was about forty pounds underweight and his rear legs didn't work very well. His ears were filled with crud, the result of years of neglect, which most likely caused his deafness. A friend managed to free Ralph from his shackles and then connected him with Deborah, whose organization provides rescue, adoption and lifelong quality care for senior dogs in need.

"Ralph was probably the gentlest dog I ever met," says Deborah. After a vet predicted the German shepherd mix was running short on time, Deborah decided to keep him, instead of trying to find an adoptive home. She remembers that Ralph didn't understand the concept of a doggie bowl when he first arrived. "I had to toss food on the ground for the first few days" in order to get him to eat. He also walked around in circles, a common restlessness for dogs that have been chained up for years. "He never quite understood he was free. His world was always a circle."

But Ralph did comprehend the tenderness and companionship of another dog with special needs. Although he couldn't hear her, and she couldn't see him, Ralph and Samantha quickly became the best of friends. "Where one was, the other was," says Deborah. They especially enjoyed snacking on pita bread together, a quite dinner for two, as it were, for the contented couple gently sharing their twilight time.

Ralph died five months after he first met Samantha; his earlier years had taken their toll. Samantha grieved. A few days after his death, Deborah took Samantha for her weekly body massage, a pleasure Ralph and Samantha indulged in together. "During her first massage treatment without him, she became agitated, broke from the therapist and ran recklessly through the house," Deborah remembers. "When I put Ralph's collar around her neck, she seemed to sense his presence and became much calmer."

Renal failure took Samantha's life six months later. Although their time together was short, it was profound and good.

"They gave me so much and asked for so little in return," says Deborah. "Ralph, my gentle, loving spirit, taught me that love can fill up all the hurt places if we only let it. And Samantha, my beautiful blind dog, taught me that seeing with the heart is the clearest vision of all."

Paddy

I t is impossible to gaze at the angelic face of the young Labrador-pit bull mix without wondering what on earth was going through the minds of the group of children hanging around the streets of Milwaukee that March afternoon. It's even harder to imagine what the twelve-week-old puppy was thinking as the youngsters tied a thick shoelace around his tiny black-and-white neck and hung him from a tree branch. His soft, soulful eyes bulged from the pain and terror as he struggled and gasped, while the kids stood there and chuckled in amusement.

The Wisconsin Humane Society considers what happened to Paddy "one of the most horrible cases of animal abuse in recent memory." It was the day before St. Patrick's Day and, although the puppy's luck had been bad, very bad, it was about to change. Three young men, two teenagers and a twenty-year-old, were driving by when they saw the youngsters congregating around a tree. They stopped to see what was going on, and the children scattered.

The rescuers showed up just in time; the puppy was still breathing. One of the young men climbed the tree and freed the victim. They rushed him to the humane society where he arrived in shock and barely conscious. "It's horrible because he had to suffer a lot of pain," explained veterinarian Randal Zeman. The initial prognosis was not good. Even if the puppy lived, there would be a significant possibility of brain damage.

"Clinging to life and starting to seizure, the puppy, later named Paddy for his survival on St. Patrick's Day, was rushed into our veterinary clinic where our veterinarians worked frantically to save his life," the humane society reports. "We were afraid the little guy wouldn't pull through. But thanks to hours of expert care, Paddy made a miraculous recovery."

The media picked up on Paddy's story and animal lovers responded with generosity and support. Nearly two dozen people asked if they could adopt the puppy. Hundreds of people donated gifts or called to wish the dog well. A local pet store offered a year's worth of food to nourish the mending animal. Financial support from society donors paid for the medical expenses and for "humane education programs to prevent similar tragedies in the future." Donors also put up a $10,000 reward for information leading to the arrest and conviction of those responsible for the crime. No one has ever been apprehended.

Less than a month after the lynching, Paddy felt just fine, and there was no sign of brain damage. The lucky puppy was adopted by Jennifer and David Carroll and moved into their home on six acres, where he runs around with their two other dogs. Despite the earlier trauma, there are no emotional scars. "He's not afraid of anyone," says Jennifer, not even kids. "He's doing quite well. He's your typical dog."

His favorite activity is chasing squirrels. After a squirrel runs up a tree, Paddy sits beneath it for a long while, staring up at the branches.

Stubby

The stray bull terrier puppy had no idea what he was signing up for the day he moseyed onto the athletic field at Yale University. He saw a bunch of young guys marching around and decided to join the fun. His new buddies turned out to be members of the 102nd Infantry Battalion of the 25th Yankee Division, and they were preparing for deployment. The year was 1917, and the new recruit with the stubby tail and brindled coat would soon be heading "over there."

Stubby hit it off with everyone in camp, especially Private J. Robert Conroy. Although policy dictated otherwise, the commander allowed Stubby to remain at the compound. When it came time to ship out, Conroy refused to say goodbye to his pet and smuggled Stubby aboard a transport truck, troop train and then into the belly of their ship that shoved off toward the Western Front.

When the Yanks landed in France, Conroy convinced his new commander of Stubby's morale value, and the dog was assigned to duty as special mascot of the 102nd. The soldiers arrived on the front lines in February 1918 and dug in for the inevitability of brutal trench warfare. Conditions were miserable in the cold, wet and muddy trenches, but the imminent danger was not at their feet. It came in the form of enemy bullets that constantly whizzed an inch or two overhead. Oftentimes, a bullet found its target.

Stubby's first battlefield injury came not from a gun, though, but instead when the Germans launched an attack using poison gas. The dog was transported to a field hospital where he fully recovered and later returned to the front. As it turned out, the incident proved fortuitous. Soon afterward, as the doughboys slept, the enemy launched an early-morning gas attack. Stubby recognized the scent and ran through the trench waking up the men in time for them to don their gas masks. Stubby saved more than one life that day.

He's also credited with helping locate and rescue wounded soldiers who became trapped in "no-man's land," the lethal real estate located between the Allied and German trenches. One of his most famous exploits involved the capture of an enemy infiltrator who hid in nearby brush while mapping out the positions of the American trenches. Stubby spotted the errant map maker who, upon seeing Stubby coming his way, turned and high-tailed it in the direction of his own trench. He wasn't fast enough, though. Stubby caught the spy, chomped down on his derriere and held him for capture. Stubby's repeated bravery earned him the respect of his fellow soldiers and a promotion to the rank of sergeant.

But World War I was far from over. During one especially brutal attack, a German grenade exploded near Stubby. Shrapnel ripped through his chest and leg. Conroy rushed his dog to the field hospital where doctors fixed him up and ordered rest and recuperation before he was allowed to return to the front lines. By the time the war ended, Stubby had survived seventeen battles. Newspapers throughout the country called him a hero. President Woodrow Wilson personally congratulated him, and Stubby returned the complement with a salute. General John "Black Jack" Pershing hung a special gold medal around Stubby's neck. The American Legion, American Red Cross and YMCA each made him an honorary member. He led more parades than perhaps any dog before or since. When World War II unfolded, the military established the K-9 Corps. Stubby, "America's first war dog," is credited with serving as an inspiration for the corps.

That might have been enough for the average dog but not Stubby. Following his enlistment, Conroy enrolled in the Georgetown University Law School, and Stubby tagged along. They both enjoyed football more than studying torts, so Conroy invited his friend to Saturday afternoon games. At halftime, Stubby ran out on the field and pushed the pigskin up and down the gridiron with his nose. Fans loved the spectacle. Georgetown named Stubby its mascot.

Sergeant Stubby, the stray from nowhere, was charmed with good luck and shared it with everyone he touched.

Mocha

Bill O'Neill Sr. climbed into warm clothes and headed out the door on a cold New England morning just after Christmas to shovel snow. At six feet, seven inches tall and weighing well over 200 pounds, Bill could make short work of the job that lay before him; he had been doing so all his life. This day, however, would be different.

As he tossed the heavy shovel into the air again and again, Bill sensed something strange. A pain shot through his chest. "This doesn't feel right," Bill thought to himself as he kept on shoveling. Maybe it was all those holiday snacks he enjoyed the day before. Recognizing there was a problem, his wife, Carol, asked if she should call someone. Bill said it wasn't necessary; he was in good health and, besides, he had no personal history of heart trouble.

A few moments later he glanced over at his dog, Mocha, a ninety-pound German shepherd mix who was about twenty-five feet away and straining at the runner like she had never done before. "She was staring at me with the weirdest, haunting look," Bill remembers. "It was spooky, as if she was telling me: *You're in trouble, pal.*" After seeing Mocha's expression and remembering an article he read about dogs and their oftentimes inexplicable connection with humans, Bill said to his wife: "Carol, call 911. The dog knows something that I don't know."

The police chief arrived within five minutes and an ambulance five minutes after that. Bill's pain grew more intense. As the ambulance raced to the hospital, rescue workers pumped medication into the big man who by now realized he was in big trouble. Doctors at the hospital discovered a ninety-nine percent blockage in one of his arteries. Bill was having a heart attack, and they needed to operate right away.

The medical team performed emergency surgery and caught the attack just in time; Bill's heart tissue suffered minimal damage. The doctor told Bill if he waited ten or fifteen minutes longer, he might have died. "I would have been stubborn and stuck it out," Bill admits, "until I looked at that dog. I was real, real lucky. I owe her quite a bit."

Although her motivation and instincts will never be understood, Mocha's action paid Bill back for saving her. He adopted the young brown-and-black dog with a "perfect disposition" from the New Hampshire Society for the Prevention of Cruelty to Animals. Described as a "sweet, big baby," Mocha was rescued from a retirement community where she had been hooked up to a harness and forced to pull residents in their wheelchairs. The harness was so tight and dug so deeply into the dog's skin, it left permanent scars.

Several days after Bill entered the hospital, he returned to his home in Kingston. Mocha "couldn't stop licking my face. She knew something had happened," he says. Two days later the entrepreneur went back to work, with his "best friend" by his side. Bill credits Mocha and everyone else who helped during his ordeal with saving his life. And he fondly remembers the day he first saw Mocha at the shelter, when she looked up at him as if to ask, "*Hey buddy, would you help me out here?*" They seem to have helped each other.

Zeke

It happened on a Sunday afternoon at a Greyhound track in Tucson. During a training race an extremely fast two-year-old, who would later be named Zeke, caught up to the electronic lure as a blur of spirited canines sped around the oval. Zeke tugged on the lure's fleece cover and it flew back into his eyes. Temporarily blinded, he slowed down as three competitors barreled into him from behind. Zeke flew over the inside rail and crashed hard onto his left side in the gravel infield. He was hurt . . . badly.

While the Arizona sun beat down on the bloodied, severely injured animal, his owners and other racing aficionados rushed to his side. It looked bad. Zeke's left leg was shattered and an artery severed. His upper and lower jaws were broken. There was a huge gash in his brindled coat, exposing the hip muscle. Several bystanders suggested the dog be put out of his misery immediately. His owners, however, wanted to see if there was an alternative.

They rushed Zeke to an emergency clinic where he was stabilized, but extensive and expensive medical work was required if he wanted to walk, let alone run, again. The owners weren't prepared for that scenario, so they contacted a Greyhound rescue organization to see if anyone was interested in saving the dog who had just overrun his own destiny.

Greyhound rescuers are a committed bunch, and word spread quickly. It reached Debi and Woody Woodman of Fast Dogs-Fast Friends Rescue and Adoption in Glendale. They co-founded the organization just three months earlier and had a total of $133.46 in the till. Zeke's vet bills were expected to climb into the thousands.

With the help of other Greyhound rescuers, they flew Zeke to a nearby veterinary hospital. "I've never seen a dog that beat-up," Debi remembers. After four and a half hours of surgery, it appeared Zeke would pull through. His left front leg, they were sorry to learn, wouldn't. It was amputated. Nonetheless, after a few weeks of recuperation, Zeke was on the mend. "He's a very, very determined dog," says Debi. The Woodmans worked with Zeke at their home where he learned to walk and run on three legs and to become a house pet. (Greyhounds spend the majority of their racing lives cooped up in small crates.) "This dog had no idea he had only three legs," Debi explains. He was doing great.

But there were still medical expenses to deal with; the final bill: $2,978. Fast Dogs-Fast Friends posted Zeke's story on its web site and donations started to arrive—five dollars here, twenty dollars there. Money came in from all over the world. People can be kind with the right motivation. Within six weeks, donations paid for all but $150 of Zeke's medical bills. Adoption inquiries also came in. With eight Greyhounds of their own, the

Woodmans started screening applicants. Soon afterward, a couple involved with Greyhound rescue who had two dogs of their own welcomed Zeke into their home and gave him a new life.

Today, Zeke is an active spokesdog for Greyhound adoptions. The healthy, happy sprinter who was once at death's door attends more than a dozen public relations events each year, including the annual Arizona Renaissance Festival where he greets thousands of well-wishers. About a year after the accident, Zeke participated in a fun-run in Utah. He was clocked at 34 miles per hour . . . on three legs. "He's an amazing dog," says Debi.

Zeke's tale is about "a bunch of people working together to save one dog," Debi explains. "But I won't be happy until all of them are saved."

❧

Daisy Mae

Neither rain, nor snow, nor pit bull ... well, maybe a pit bull. Letter carriers have their hands full all day long. The last thing they need to contend with is an aggressive, perhaps misunderstood, dog. But an incident of that nature occurred one summer in the Berkshire Mountains of Massachusetts.

A solid black Labrador retriever-pit bull mix tied outside a home was threatening the postman and others. It barked and lunged at the letter carrier during rounds. The dog, later named Daisy Mae, also frightened some people in the neighborhood. The postmaster complained to the local selectmen. Given the circumstances, the town fathers ordered the owner to keep the dog confined and secured when no one was home. For whatever reason, the owner refused. Citations were issued. Still, nothing happened. The local newspaper picked up the story, and Daisy Mae's notoriety spread. Action was about to be taken.

Daisy Mae ended up in the dog pound. She wasn't thrilled to be there and initially displayed more aggression. For a dog that is taken into custody, good behavior is essential if there is to be any hope for adoption. On the other hand, a dog that's been tied up outside for long periods of time without attention tends to lose its manners. Daisy Mae's days were numbered.

"Most of the selectmen are dog owners," one of them explained. "Having to put the dog down was an absolutely last resort. That was an agonizing decision, but we had to think about the safety of the neighborhood."

Perhaps the only chance for Daisy Mae came when the animal control officer phoned Bonnie Bassis, owner of A Place for Us, Bonnie's Foster Home for Dogs in South Egremont. Bonnie takes dogs from shelters, up to four at a time, socializes them and allows them to live as members of the family until a permanent home can be found. She has a fondness for pit bulls, an often maligned breed.

The interim guests "sleep in cushioned crates in several bedrooms and have the run of the house," explains Bonnie. "Two dog doors, various gates, two separate living quarters, an acre and a half of above-ground fencing, as well as invisible fencing make life almost ideal for everyone, except for my three cats who wish this fostering nonsense would just stop."

When Bonnie picked up Daisy Mae, who had already calmed down a bit for the animal control officer, she discovered "one of the sweetest dogs imaginable." She adapted immediately to the good life at A Place for Us and was soon ready for adoption.

Bonnie found a grandmother who wanted a dog, and the pair clicked. No longer tethered to her past, the infamous Daisy Mae, who once threatened an entire neighborhood, now lives the quiet life at her new home in the countryside. "They're doing absolutely wonderfully, and the dog is great with her two young grandchildren," Bonnie reports.

"Daisy Mae was tied outside and not given a chance to be a dog. Once she had that chance, she just blossomed," says Bonnie. "That's true with so many dogs."

Chester

Some dogs demonstrate greater affection than others, just like people, only dogs are more sincere. Chester was a loving dog. He was about six months old when he turned up at the Free To Live no-kill animal sanctuary in Edmond, Oklahoma. No one remembers how or why he arrived; it was a long time ago.

His pedigree was uncertain but definitely contained some schipperke. Pure black with short legs and weighing about forty-five pounds, Chester blended in with the other dogs at the sanctuary. When prospective adopters came a looking, they never seemed to notice Chester. So he spent his first six years playing with canine companions, many of whom moved on to new homes over time, and snuggling with staff members and volunteers when it was his turn for attention. Executive Director Ron Wingler remembers the kisses Chester gave him whenever they met. "He was very friendly," says Ron. Life was good for Chester, but with all that pent up affection, he really needed to be part of a family.

One day his wish came true. He was adopted by an Oklahoma City couple who saw in Chester what others had not. They took him home and all went well for a few days until Chester dug a hole under their fence and took off. The family and Ron looked high and low, but Chester was nowhere to be found. Everyone worried. After more than a week of searching, it looked as though the sweet and gentle dog was gone for good.

A few days later Ron received a phone call from a stranger saying there was a black dog with a Free To Live tag lying in grass off a roadway at a busy cloverleaf intersection halfway between the sanctuary and Oklahoma City. The caller was out hunting for his own lost dog and spotted Chester, who had evidently been trying to make his way back to Free To Live, approximately fifteen miles away. How he figured out the route is "one of the dog mysteries of life," says Ron.

"I jumped in my car and sped to the location in hopes of finding him alive," explains Ron. "Sure enough, there he was, and when I called his name, those great funnel ears perked up. He was very glad to hear an old friend's voice."

But the stress of Chester's nearly two-week ordeal and the sudden and unexpected onset of a rare disease rendered him very ill. He was nearly blind and had lost most of the mobility in his back legs. Ron took Chester to four veterinarians before he was finally diagnosed. By then he was totally blind. If he lived, which was doubtful, his rear legs would probably not work. Each vet suggested that Chester be put to sleep.

"I had been visiting him regularly during his hospitalization, but when I got this news, I was almost ready to give up. It was during that visit that Chester and I made an agreement, a partnership of sorts," explains Ron. "He was very weak and could barely raise his head, but I promised that if he would get better, I would take him home with me and take care of him. His head slowly raised off the blanket and those wonderful funnel ears perked up. I swear to this day he understood what I was saying."

Much to everyone's surprise and delight, Chester recovered. It took seven or eight months of exercises and heavy doses of antibiotics, but he finally gained some mobility in his legs. The rear limbs were never quite right, but he could walk again and "almost run." Because of the health problems, the adoptive family agreed it would be best if Ron kept Chester.

"Although he was never able to see, this guy was able to maneuver around like crazy, and during the whole time of his recovery he was happy and never complained," Ron explains. "I remember a few times when I was having a bad day, I would look at Chester and realize I had no reason to gripe."

Ron and Chester enjoyed nearly five years together until the aging dog's kidneys started to fail. "Even on his deathbed, when I would come home, he would make every possible effort to greet me at the door. One Sunday morning in October he made one final attempt to reach me and passed away quietly at my side," Ron remembers. "His outlook on life was wonderful, always happy, just glad to be alive and with someone he loved."

Muffin

L ittle old Muffin survived—by a whisker—the ultimate doggy nightmare: she lived alone in a house with eighteen adult cats. It gets worse . . . much worse.

A woman who cared for pets in her own peculiar way rented a house in rural Minnesota and settled in with her gang of felines and a lone Lhasa apso, Muffin. This type of eccentric lifestyle occurs here and there throughout the country, sometimes successfully, other times not. One day in October the woman moved out, leaving the dog and cats behind, shut inside a cold, empty house without adequate food or water.

October turned to November, November to December, as the snow fell and the temperature dropped. Christmas and New Year Year's passed without celebration. Living conditions festered. The house turned into one big litter box. Whatever food or water might have been there was long gone. None of the cats, mostly purebreds, was spayed or neutered. Each one's nine lives wasted away faster than ice freezes during a Minnesota winter.

Muffin somehow managed to blend in with the others, but the desperate situation took its toll. The animals were starving to death; some were sick. They couldn't last

61

much longer. Finally, in January, a relative of the woman discovered the animals and drove them to Contented Critters Animal Sanctuary in Makinen. When sanctuary founder Faye Peters and her husband, Walter, first saw Muffin, they were aghast. "It was so matted and there was so much hair and so much feces, you couldn't tell if it was a dog," Faye remembers. "You couldn't tell the front from the back . . . if it was male or female."

A groomer quickly came and shaved off the shaggy, filthy mementos of Muffin's horrible ordeal. Then a veterinarian administered an I.V., lay on the sanctuary floor and fed Muffin chicken and rice, one spoonful at a time. "She had forgotten how to eat," says Faye. "The vet said that within 24 hours the dog would have died." Muffin rested on a recliner for several weeks and ate tiny bits of hand-fed food as she tried to regain her strength. "It was touch and go," says Faye. "We didn't know if she was going to make it or not." Muffin had totally lost her hearing but, hopefully, not her will to live.

One day a young woman stopped by the sanctuary and saw the listless dog lying down, still in rough shape, and tears came to her eyes. Filled with sympathy and purpose, she asked Faye: "Can I take her home with me? Dad needs her." Faye was somewhat reluctant. "Do you know what you're getting into?" she asked. The young woman did, indeed, and since Faye knew the family, she agreed to let Muffin go.

Muffin left the sanctuary and embarked on the best years of her life. She still didn't have the strength to stand up to eat, and had to be fed by hand for quite some time, but eventually the ten-year-old girl recovered, except for her hearing. She and the young woman's father became "thick as thieves." They were inseparable, an older man and an older dog, sharing each other's company at their own pace, in their own way. "She was more than a dog to him," says Faye, "she was a friend."

Muffin still thought about the cats from time to time and was happy to learn they all lived and ended up in good homes. Maybe, just maybe, those earlier days were all a bad dream.

Kirby

Kirby is a very smart dog who has reached out to millions of people throughout the country with a message of grave importance: neuter and spay your dogs and cats. Pet overpopulation is an enormously sad affliction that could, and should, be overcome.

Kirby was a stray nine- or ten-week-old puppy scampering around Connecticut with his three siblings when animal control officers picked them up. Healthy and adorable, they were taken to the Animal Welfare Society, a no-kill shelter in New Milford, and put up for adoption. At the same time, a local photographer was involved with a project for the United States Postal Service, looking for just the right faces to adorn two new 37-cent, first-class stamps that would promote neutering and spaying.

The Australian shepherd-collie-border collie mix and a kitten named Samantha, both shelter residents, proved to be the perfect models. They behaved as well as can be expected during the photo shoot, which resulted in the post office printing 250 million of the stamps and issuing them September 20, 2002, at the annual conference of the American Humane Association. Kirby's wistful face is featured on one stamp, Samantha's on the other. Appearing along the top of a sheet of twenty stamps is the notice: "Too many animals. Too few homes. Save lives. Neuter or spay."

"I'm delighted that the postal service is leading this new effort to raise public awareness of the importance of neutering or spaying companion animals to help prevent pet overpopulation and help avoid health and behavioral problems," says Dr. Virginia Noelke, chairperson of the Citizen Stamp Advisory Committee. Eight to ten million dogs and cats enter shelters each year in the United States. Four to five million unwanted animals are euthanized annually.

"Spaying your female dog or cat virtually eliminates her chance of developing a uterine infection, uterine cancer and ovarian cancer, and reduces the possibility that she might develop breast cancer," explains Dr. Joe Howell, president of the American Veterinary Medical Association. "Neutering male dogs and cats will eliminate the possibility of testicular cancer, help prevent some diseases of the prostate and can sometimes help reduce aggression. Spaying or neutering your pet can also make them less likely to roam, run away or get into fights."

Soon after his modeling career concluded, Kirby was adopted, as were his siblings and Samantha. He now lives a quite, unassuming life with a family in Connecticut, where he romps in the yard, rides in the car, goes hiking and camping, and plays all day with his house mates: several young cats. With his roaming days behind him, the former stray is reportedly well behaved and very happy. He's also neutered. Smart dog.

ᦂᦂᦂ

Mamma

Mamma was "just about starved to death" when she arrived at Casey's Habit Purebred Shelter in Conway, Missouri. The nine-year-old pug had been abandoned along a gravel road two weeks earlier. Jackie and Bill French, who operate the small, family-run rescue together with their three children, believe Mamma drank from mud puddles and scavenged whatever she could to stay alive.

A family friend found the trembling brown-and-black purebred with widespread toes wandering like a lost lamb and took her to the shelter. Mamma was an emaciated, dehydrated mess, but the French family immediately started nursing her back to health with the help of a local vet.

During an examination they discovered a tattoo that helped uncover answers to the dog's past. Mamma had been a breeding bitch. Her toes mutated because she lived in a wire mesh cage throughout her life—even the floor was made of wire, reminiscent of a large chicken coop. Paws aren't designed to walk, day in and day out, along thin metal strands raised above the ground.

When Mamma's services were no longer required, she was sold at a breeder's auction. Soon after she was sold at another auction, and then another—four auctions in six months. Breeding is big business in that neck of the woods. Some breeders have excellent reputations; others are not so affectionately known as "puppy mills." None, however, seemed to want an aging puppy machine like Mamma.

Finally, the last breeder gave Mamma away to a young family who wanted a dog. Problem was, Mamma wasn't housebroken. Dogs who are kept in cages their entire lives rarely are. Unable to cope with a difficult period of potty training, the father of the family drove Mamma to a secluded spot and dumped her out of the car. Living most of her days in a cage was bad enough for the friendly little dog, but abandonment along a lonely roadway must have felt like the terrifying conclusion to what had been a less-than-perfect existence.

Mamma had just struck bottom. Life, however, was about to improve.

It took three months of devotion and caring to "get Mamma back on her feet," Jackie explains. If they were to find Mamma a new home, the French family knew they would have to work on housebreaking her as well. They kept at it, lavishing Mamma with praise when she got it right.

Eventually they decided Mamma was adoptable, so they put out the word and several people responded. One was a young woman whose middle-aged mother was in a wheelchair, the result of a car accident. She needed a companion. A meeting was planned. Could it be that after all those years without affection, Mamma was finally about to experience the love she deserved? As soon as they met, the woman "hauled her up into her lap and Mamma was just as content as could be," Jackie remembers. "They were meant to be together. They're doing wonderfully."

⁓

BJ

BJ kept pawing at Rob's arm. It was an early morning in May, and Rob had fallen asleep only a few hours before. He figured BJ wanted to go out but hoped the Australian-shepherd mix could hold on a while longer. As Rob drifted through drowsiness, BJ's anxiety increased; he insisted that Rob get up. The tenacity paid off—Rob pulled himself out of bed and followed the young dog he and his wife, Angela, adopted a month earlier from the Kansas Humane Society. But instead of heading for the door, BJ made a beeline for their daughter, Ashley's, room.

BJ came to live with the Neises family because of Ashley. The precious twenty-month-old suffered from cerebral palsy, and her neurologist agreed that a dog might provide needed stimulation. Rob and Angela already wanted a dog, and when the doctor confirmed that a pet could be a positive addition to the family, the only thing left was the challenge of finding the right one.

They searched for months and then learned of a service dog program affiliated with the humane society that had three candidates: two German shepherds and BJ. Rob and Angela first selected one of the shepherds, but it became immediately clear the dog was wrong for Ashley. BJ, on the other hand, held promise. "He took an

69

interest in Ashley," Angela says. A mutt with two different colored eyes and long floppy ears, BJ wasn't as noble as the purebred, but he was extremely gentle, loving and expressed a real fondness for the little girl. "We decided then and there to take him home," the parents explain.

It took about a week for BJ to settle into his new life as a family dog. He was very sweet and laid back but also loved to play, often rambunctiously, with adults. When it came to Ashley, however, he instinctively knew to calm down and be careful. "He sensed what we felt," says Angela. BJ also tried his best to protect Ashley. He ran and sat by her side when she coughed or gasped for breath as a result of her severe disability.

As Rob followed the determined BJ into Ashley's bedroom that fateful spring morning, there was no coughing or gasping. Instead, Rob walked into a parent's worst nightmare—his daughter was asphyxiating. She lay in the crib with her head covered in blankets, and her young life was draining away. Rob scooped up his daughter and together with his wife rushed her to a nearby hospital. They made it in time. Ashley recovered and was able to return home in a few days.

Mom and dad are certain BJ saved their daughter's life. "He knew something was wrong," says Angela. "We're so grateful for him." Just how this once-abandoned shelter dog, who now and then acts a little "goofy," understood the gravity of that particular situation is unclear. Was it his intelligence? Instinct? Divine intervention? Dogs are known for their unconditional love. That might have been enough.

Chance & Hope

The adorable puppy's little legs moved faster than a slithering rattlesnake. She hurried forward then looked back, urging the man and woman to follow. They spotted the puppy all alone in the desert and tried to catch her, but she wasn't willing to be caught; there was something on her mind. As the August sun seared the rocks and tumbleweed of the desolate New Mexico mesa, the hikers finally discovered the reason for her anxiety.

They found the puppy's mother lying in the dust, encrusted in dried blood. At least two or three days earlier, someone shot the older dog and then kicked the puppy squarely and solidly in the jaw. Both animals were left to bake in the desert, injured and helpless. Whoever meant to kill them was too lazy to finish the job or, perhaps, enjoyed the idea of the red heelers suffering for a while before they died. It turned out to be a botched execution either way. The dogs managed to survive until the hikers stumbled upon the puppy.

The victims were taken to the Animal Humane Association of New Mexico where a veterinarian operated on the gunshot wound. Unfortunately, it was severe, and the mother's left hind leg had to be amputated. "There was no chance to save it," says shelter volunteer Kathy

Newman. "I can't imagine anybody doing what they did to her." Later it was discovered that the puppy's jaw was broken, but surgery was not an option. The injury would have to mend on its own.

The dogs "were a mess" when they arrived at the shelter. Both were filthy and needed a good meal; mom was very skinny. Although they looked like a pair of wounded waifs, they were sweet, well behaved, and perfectly mannered.

Kathy first saw the mother the day after surgery. She wore a large Elizabethan-style collar, so as not to chew open her stitches, and was already up and walking on three legs. As Kathy bent down to see the patient's face, the dog looked up and kissed her. "That was it," explains Kathy, who immediately decided to adopt her. "For a dog to go through what she went through," she deserved a good home. As for the little one? "If the puppy had done that for mom, how could you separate them?"

In fact, the dogs had been apart in the safety of the shelter for a week. Mother and daughter were reunited on the day they left for their new home, and the affection they displayed when they first saw each other choked up more than one seasoned humane society member. "It was the most wonderful thing I've ever seen," remembers Kathy. "We were all crying. The love and bond they have for each other is just amazing."

Both mother (named Chance) and daughter (Hope) moved in with Kathy, her blue heeler and Australian shepherd. "They're doing wonderfully," says Kathy. Chance regained the weight she lost, possibly because she's become something of a couch potato, and the puppy grew to be bigger than her three senior house mates. The dogs play together, go for walks, and sometimes run around in the mountains. Chance has been known to run faster, on three legs, than the others when she feels like it.

These dogs are living proof that each morning as the sun greets a new day of human folly, there's a chance that good people will override evil deeds. There's always hope.

❦

Torch

This dog's perceived faults turned out to be his saving grace. The eight-month-old Labrador-pointer mix was a handful. Originally named Rascal, he exploded with energy, played as hard and as often as he could, and wouldn't listen worth a darn. It didn't take long for Rascal's owners to realize the rambunctious pet was too much for them to deal with, so they surrendered him to Saint Hubert's Animal Welfare Center in New Jersey.

The friendly, chocolate-colored mutt had a hard time calming down there, too. Volunteer coaches worked with him for weeks on obedience skills, but his extreme enthusiasm caused prospective adopters to hightail it when they witnessed his exuberance. "We did everything we could to help Rascal run off his energy, but no matter how much time we ran him outside, he seemed to go stir crazy in the kennel," says shelter staff member Anna Mae Allison. "He thrashed his tail so hard against the kennel wall that it bled."

High-energy, overly playful dogs rarely make it to the top of the average adopter's wish list, but Frank Abbate had something special in mind when he contacted Saint Hubert's North Branch shelter. Frank, an inspector with the New Brunswick (New Jersey) Fire Department, needed a dog, quickly—one with characteristics that suggested it could be trained to be an arson detector. Experts who train scent dogs often prefer an animal with a heightened play drive. They redirect the dog's energy and playfulness into its work, melding enthusiasm with the canine's extraordinary sense of smell in order to detect various substances, such as flammable liquids, narcotics or explosives. Saint Hubert's, it turned out, had the ideal candidate.

When Frank met Torch, the dog tilted his head and looked inquisitively into Frank's eyes, like dogs do in the movies. There was an immediate connection. "He was like a ball of fire," says Frank. Hence, the new name, Torch. "He was perfect."

The puppy also turned out to be a quick study; he had no choice. Frank and a different dog had just started an arson training program with the state police. Sadly, that dog was killed by a truck the day after the first class, leaving Frank with a weekend to find a new dog who could measure up. Not a problem for Torch. After less than two days of preparation, he amazed everyone at the academy the morning he arrived with his innate abilities. He was born to be a scent dog.

The fire inspector and his new partner spent four hundred hours training together, learning how to become an arson detection team. Torch can now sniff out eighteen different flammable substances, before and after they've burned. Even before he graduated, Torch helped solve the case of a suspicious garage fire. Frank took Torch to the scene and the arson-dog-in-training quickly found a pile of charred clothing that turned out to have been doused in lighter fluid and set afire by a youngster. Since then, Torch has assisted in scores of arson investigations. More than one arsonist woke up behind bars thanks to Torch.

In addition to solving crimes, Torch regularly goes on the road with Frank to schools, hospitals and civic groups to teach fire prevention. During the presentation to children, Frank tells Torch's story, how he was once criticized for his behavior, but then how he learned to channel his energy into something positive. "He's a special dog," says Frank. The inspector teaches the kids that they, too, have special abilities that can be used constructively. Because of his outstanding accomplishments, Torch was inducted into the New Jersey Veterinary Medical Association's Hall of Fame. The group recognizes animals who exemplify the strength of the bond between animals and humans.

cakao

Spanky

Spanky thinks he's a dog. He chases the cat, begs for food at the kitchen table, plays with the family dogs, sleeps with his arms wrapped around their warm, furry bodies. . . . Not only does he *think* he's cut from a canine cloth, "he's *sure* he's a dog," says Frances "Kitten" Jones of Lighthouse Animal Rescue in Edgewater, Florida. The thing is, Spanky's a cat, a short-hair tabby who has every right to harbor identity issues, especially after all he's been through.

When Spanky was just five months old, a teenager doused the adorable striped kitten with a flammable liquid and set him on fire. By all rights, Spanky should have died but, instead, he wobbled through the neighborhood for some seven days before sitting down to rest on a porch one cold night in January. A woman spotted the severely injured animal, believed it had been hit by a car, and called Lighthouse.

Frances and her husband, Bruce, responded. "I could see the cat on the doorstep all hunkered over, and the first thought that came to my mind was, it's been burned," Frances remembers. "As I got closer to him, I could see the skin on his back—from his neck to his tail—was curled up and away from his body, like fried meat skin. One ear was hanging by a couple of hairs, and the other ear had crumbled." She approached the cat slowly as those around her warned, "don't touch him." Then Frances kneeled down and spoke softly and reassuringly to the badly wounded and frightened kitten. "He immediately raised his head, came to me and started rubbing against me." She petted him under his chin and belly, the only spots that appeared safe to touch. "He was all over me," says Frances. "He knew someone had come to help."

Frances and Bruce drove the kitten to their home, fed him and gave him water to drink. "He was starving," says Frances. Surprisingly, the kitten didn't appear to be in any pain, despite the fact that much of his skin was burned off completely, exposing muscle and bone. While Spanky wolfed down the food, Frances managed to cut off some of the loose, dead skin and the one ear that dangled by a thread. She feared he would rip the skin off himself, causing further injury. Frances dabbed salve on the wounds, wrapped Spanky in a loose bandage, and placed him in a warm crate. It was Friday night, and they wouldn't make it to a vet until Monday. If the doctor suggested Spanky was suffering and the prognosis bleak, they would put him to sleep. Otherwise, they felt he deserved a fighting chance.

Spanky spent the next two to three weeks with the veterinarian, undergoing surgery, including the removal of his other ear, and various procedures in the effort to save his life. "He went through quite a bit," says Frances. When he was well enough, Spanky moved in with

Frances, Bruce and their house filled with rescued dogs, where he recuperated in a crate for another month.

After Spanky's skin regenerated and his health improved, Frances decided it was time to let the kitten out to play for brief periods. She introduced Spanky to her most affable animal, an American Eskimo dog named Buddy, and they hit it off from the get-go. "Spanky had a ball," says Frances. Gradually, the little kitten with no ears became friendly with the other dogs, from twelve to twenty canines at any given time. "He grew up in a house full of dogs," says Frances. "He's not your ordinary cat."

Today, at four years old, Spanky the grown-up cog (politically correct term for a cat with canine tendencies) enjoys himself fully as a fellow pack member at Lighthouse. Considering the cruelty he suffered, it's remarkable that Spanky adjusted so well. "He had such a strong will to live," says Frances. "He did not want to die." Courage prevails in different forms, different species.

꒰ꕤ꒱

Angus

Blind and alone, the miniature schnauzer sniffed and bumped his way around a small North Carolina town, trying his best to find a scrap of food, a drink of water and a safe place to lie down and rest on a cold winter night. Once he had a home, he was someone's pet, but that seemed like a long time ago. Now he was all by himself, a stray who could see only shades of light and dark and had nothing to rely on but his own inner resolve.

When Angus finally arrived at Happy Hills Animal Foundation in Staley, he was matted and road-weary but was an absolute sweetheart. He charmed everyone at the no-kill shelter, which made the people there even more determined to find him a good home—although they recognized he wasn't the most adoptable dog to come down the pike.

"Over the next couple of months, Angus demonstrated what a wonderful dog he was," the shelter reports. "He was already housebroken, walked great on a leash, and was good with adults, children, other dogs, even puppies. He was briefly adopted by a local man but returned when the man's other male dog just wouldn't accept him."

On the other side of the country, a family in Washington with three schnauzers was ready to adopt another. They found Angus on the Happy Hills' website and, after several weeks of consideration, a decision drifted out of the twilight and into their hearts. "That night I dreamed about Angus," explains Dale. "I saw him here. I saw him smiling. And I realized with absolute clarity that the someone Angus was waiting for was us."

No one was thrilled with the idea of putting a blind dog in the bottom of a jet and flying him cross-country, but the trip went smoothly, except for the many tears that flowed when the people at Happy Hills said goodbye to their little friend. Meanwhile, Dale, Ellaine and their dogs Joey, Fitz and Pip waited anxiously for the new arrival at the Seattle airport. "I practically ripped the crate containing our boy from the arms of the attendant who brought him through the double doors in the baggage claim area," Dale remembers. "We immediately opened the crate door and scooped him up into our arms."

After several days and a few bumps here and there, Angus grew accustomed to his new home. He explored inside and out, played with his schnauzer pals, and received lots of attention from Dale and Ellaine. One of his favorite outdoor activities included running along the beach at Puget Sound, splashing in the water and barking at the waves; great fun, even without the benefit of sight.

"So our life with Angus took on a routine that was comfortable for him and for us," says Dale. "He was a joy to watch because he was so happy. He didn't care that he couldn't see."

That, however, was about to change. A local veterinarian suggested that the dog's cataracts could be removed. Dale agreed to take her three-year-old dog to an ophthalmologist in Seattle. He told them there was an eighty percent chance the surgery would be successful. After much contemplation and discussion, they decided to go for it.

"Surgery day arrived and Angus and I were on our way to Seattle early in the morning," explains Dale. "After we arrived there was a long waiting period. Finally it was time and I reluctantly handed Angus over. For the next hour I walked the neighborhood. I'd brought a book to read, but I kept reading the same paragraph over and over again."

When the surgery ended, they carried the sleeping patient to Dale. "They'd wrapped him in a towel so he wouldn't get the chills as the anesthetic wore off. So I took my precious bundle . . . and held him until he began to stir," she remembers. Through a post-operative blur, Angus looked up and saw the loving face of his companion for the first time.

It took a little while for Angus to adjust to the world of vision. Everything had a new perspective. But soon he could spot birds in flight, marvel at their ascent and revel in his own.

✌

Noodles

Noodles symbolizes the reason why Animal Friends no-kill shelter in Pittsburgh opens its doors each day. This gentle, loving creature who was down on her luck had value, and she deserved human compassion.

No one knows where Noodles came from or what her life was like before animal control officers picked her up as a stray on a warm day in July. Her thick, golden-brown, chow-retriever coat desperately needed to spend some time with a bottle of shampoo and a tub full of water. Although the unkempt, aging lady appeared relatively healthy, a visit to the veterinarian was in order. The medical exam produced bad news, though. A malignant tumor grew on the back of her tongue.

"Noodles was not suffering, but the prognosis was guarded," explains Animal Friends' Linda Holsing. "Her time with us became more special, every moment more precious."

Everyone at the shelter fell in love with Noodles, and the dog reciprocated. During working hours, she could be found relaxing in the office of shelter behaviorist Kathy Reck along with her friend, Winkle, another older shelter dog. When the mood struck, the pair wandered out of the room to socialize, despite the wooden gate that was there to keep them confined. Noodles chewed through three gates before someone decided to test something sturdier. A metal gate was installed. Noodles quickly figured out how to open it and then taught Winkle the technique. Dogs will be dogs.

With time at a premium, Noodles made the most of her days. She launched a career as an eyeglass model for an optical store that features local celebrities in its advertisements. She was the first animal to earn that distinction. The ads brought her local fame, but Noodles kept it all in perspective. She would always smile and wag that bushy tail whenever a fan stopped to say hello. She demonstrated the same friendliness and enthusiasm when she visited nursing homes on pet therapy visits. On quiet, sunny days, schedule permitting, Noodles basked in the sunshine in the courtyard behind the shelter with Winkle and other senior dogs.

Life was good for Noodles through the fall and early winter, but by February the cancer had advanced to the point where a sad but inevitable decision had to be made.

Linda explained the final act of love beautifully in a tribute she wrote for Noodles: "On her last day, Noodles was surrounded by everyone who had come to love her during her stay at the shelter. This late winter day was warm, and she rested contentedly in the sunshine of the courtyard. At times there was a line of people waiting to give her one last kiss and a loving pat goodbye. Tears flowed endlessly that day. Volunteer Dan Lenz carried Noodles in a warm blanket to Kathy's car, kissing her on the forehead as he said goodbye. Kathy and volunteer

Steve Stoehr were with Noodles at the vet's office to the end. She laid her head in Kathy's hands and quietly and painlessly went to sleep.

"Noodles, we all love you and miss you. We know that there weren't any gates you had to chew through to get to the Rainbow Bridge. If we close our eyes, we can see you there, eating spaghetti with a crooked little dog named Perry, chasing after all of the angel cats and sleeping in the eternal sunshine."

Noodles leaves behind an important legacy. She came out of nowhere and touched the hearts of everyone she met. Her last months were filled with happiness and purpose, and her life came to an end in compassion's gentle embrace. There's immeasurable value in the animal-human connection.

Cooper

C ooper is going on a bear hunt, but not in the traditional sense. There are no guns involved, no killing. This is a scientific adventure with a former shelter dog pointing the way toward ecological scholarship in southeast Alaska.

When he was surrendered to the Animal Shelter of the Wood River Valley in Idaho, it was clear that one-and-a-half-year-old Cooper was energetic, friendly and very fond of chasing balls, not surprising for a Chesapeake Bay retriever-German short-haired pointer mix. "He's very affectionate and an amazing dog," says his owner and mentor, Amber Bethe. "I can't believe someone gave him up."

Cooper had lived with a family with two small children. Evidently, the kids didn't hit it off with the dog, and he was left outside quite a bit. Finally, he was taken to the shelter and put up for adoption.

At about the same time, Amber was looking for a dog to help with a project she is working on for her master's degree at Idaho State University. The graduate student is studying bear population ecology, research that involves bear population growth and/or shrinkage, territorial patterns and migration, bear relationships, and other stuff that is far too complicated for this author to understand, much less explain. Her methodology includes non-invasive genetic sampling—collecting and studying bear hair and feces. That's where Cooper comes into the picture.

Tracking down bear feces at Klondike Gold Rush National Historical Park is not necessarily as hard as finding precious nuggets in the middle of rugged grandeur, but it's certainly time consuming and tedious. For Cooper, however, it should be a breeze. He's in training now, sniffing out balls sprinkled with bear feces in order to make the association with the wild animal droppings when he gets to the north woods.

Amber interviewed a number of dogs before she met Cooper. At first she wasn't certain he was the right candidate, so she took him home to foster before making a final decision. "He seemed to have a strong drive," says Amber. "He learned so fast. I decided to take a chance, and I'm glad I did."

Cooper and Amber will spend two summers in Alaska researching the populations of both brown and black bears. This specific work in this region has never been done before. It will be quite an accomplishment for a young dog whose family believed he wasn't worth keeping.

⁂

Sophie

S pread your wings, Liza Doolittle, it's Sophie's turn on the Big Apple stage. The fictional character from *My Fair Lady,* who transformed from a street lass to a respectable young woman, has nothing over this real-life street dog from New York City. Sophie converted from an aggressive, nearly euthanized puppy into a certified therapy dog who, among other things, helped calm traumatized humans at Ground Zero after 9/11.

Animal control officers first captured the feral six-week-old border collie-sled dog mix in a drainage ditch in the Bronx, and she didn't go quietly. Sophie hated to be held by adults and screamed and nipped like a wild little banshee whenever someone picked her up. It was clear that a dog like that had no chance of being adopted, so before too long, Sophie was one stop away from the end of the line.

That's when Dr. Stephanie LaFarge, a psychologist and senior director of counseling services at the American Society for the Prevention of Cruelty to Animals, and other staff members decided to see if they could take this young, ill-mannered creature, who was clearly not suited for human cohabitation, and turn her around. It would require patience, loving care and skilled treatment.

"Sophie was a product of a horrible environment that was certainly no fault of her own," says Dr. LaFarge. "I knew it would take time, but I wanted to give her a chance." The pair spent the next several months together. During the day, the dog stayed in the doctor's office; at night they both slept there. The effort paid off. "She became more and more socialized."

Sophie did so well, if fact, that Dr. LaFarge decided to incorporate the dog into the ASPCA's intervention program for offenders who are convicted of animal abuse. "The majority of animals are harmed as the result of friction between humans," explains Dr. LaFarge. "By introducing Sophie in sessions, we can really work through people's emotions more effectively."

With a "mind of her own," Sophie maintains "an edge" during counseling that helps abusers express their feelings. She responds positively to them and vice versa. Some abusers find it meaningful to apologize to Sophie for the harm they inflicted on other animals. "Sophie has been absolutely central to the program," explains Dr. LaFarge. Animal abuse can be a marker for future violence. A number of convicted mass murderers, for example, have admitted to torturing animals before they moved on to people.

As a therapy dog, Sophie works in different capacities. After the 9/11 tragedy, she was one of the animals that helped out at Ground Zero. The alert, dedicated, white mutt with tan markings, who once had no use at all for people, found herself providing comfort to firemen, policemen, construction workers, and family members of victims who were doing their best to make it through a very trying time.

Recognizing her dramatic turnaround and all she has done to help people in need, Sophie received the ASPCA Trooper Award for animal heroism. "When I think back, I find it so ironic that Sophie is bringing such joy to others' lives today," says Dr. LaFarge. "I have learned so much from her, and it is only fair that I share her with as many people as I can."

It took a bit of doing, but Sophie is respectable now, and she's done a thousand things she'd never done before.

Hoover

They called him Pedro back on the island when he was a scruffy, homeless mutt whose future held little promise. Now he's known as Hoover, a comfortable, well-groomed New Englander who enjoys sunset cruises aboard the family boat. Hoover's fortunes changed course dramatically because of the ongoing efforts of a group of people who try their best to improve the existence of the unfortunate street dogs of Puerto Rico known as "satos."

Pedro was a sato, living day to day beneath the tropical sun in the Caribbean getaway, where basics such as food, shelter and medical care were as hard to come by for the young dog as an ace-high straight-flush in a San Juan casino. Then one day Pedro hit a lucky streak—he was picked up by a volunteer from the Save A Sato Foundation, a local organization dedicated to helping homeless and abused animals in Puerto Rico. Their task is formidable. Stray and feral dogs roam the countryside—always hungry, sometimes sick or injured, rarely spayed or neutered.

Thousands of fortunate satos have escaped their fate, however, and have been treated to a new life on mainland USA. Hoover is one of them. He arrived in Massachusetts by plane with twenty to thirty colleagues one evening, part of a program run by Animal Shelter Inc. of Sterling. Several years earlier, the shelter recognized a demand for small, adoptable dogs and subsequently joined forces with the Save A Sato Foundation. It turned out to be a win-win for adoptive families and homeless dogs.

After he arrived, Pedro took a trip to the veterinarian for shots and neutering and then went up for adoption. Despite his *"I'm-having-a-bad-hair-day"* appearance, he found a home quickly, according to Leigh Grady, the shelter director, who describes the cream-colored dog with the "big, black wet nose" as "part cocker spaniel, part jack russell terrier and part crocodile." It seems the newly arrived one-year-old enjoyed mouthing and gobbling all the paraphernalia in sight. "He's like a vacuum cleaner," says Leigh.

Pedro's new owners were overjoyed when they took him home from the shelter but soon faced a crisis. The little dog became very sick, and a veterinarian told them he would die. Distraught, they called Leigh, who assured them not to worry; she had seen sato dogs become ill before, and the problems were minor. They weren't sure who to believe but agreed to take the dog to the shelter's veterinarian. It was a good decision. Pedro's illness turned out to be a minor intestinal bug, and he recovered in a few days. That's when they named him Hoover.

Today, Hoover is as lighthearted and healthy as a youngster loose in an amusement park. He runs around the house hiding bones here and there, maintains a box filled with squeaky plastic gadgets, and loves to harass his housemate, a twenty-five pound cat. Luckily, the cat is fairly tolerant. "When his parents come home, he has a toy in his mouth and he's wagging his tail," says Leigh. "He likes to run around and be happy. He never would have that option if he was in Puerto Rico."

Someone might wonder why Sterling accepts dogs from Puerto Rico when there are so many unwanted animals closer by. "Why do they deserve any less care and love than the dogs in our area?" Leigh responds. "Who are we to say which dog deserves to live and which one deserves to die?"

❧

Pumpkin

Laura and Sara Braeutigam heard a door open and then someone talking downstairs over the din of their three dogs, who were inside the house and barking like crazy. The commotion seemed strange to the teenagers. They had been home alone for less than an hour and expected their parents, Rita and John, to arrive soon. But when they looked outside into the darkness, neither parent's car was in the driveway. Laura quickly dialed her mother's cell phone. "Mom, where are you?" she asked anxiously. "If you and dad aren't home, then someone else is in the house."

Mom and dad were at a car dealership fifteen minutes away. The enjoyment of picking up John's birthday present immediately turned to alarm. While the parents raced home, Laura telephoned the police and then a neighbor. The girls shut themselves in a bedroom, fearful of what might happen next. The dogs remained downstairs barking and growling at the intruders. Suddenly, the door burst open and Brittany, their retriever mix, flew into the bedroom to check on the girls. Their miniature Schnauzer, Alex, and Pumpkin, a young chow mix, held their ground.

Pumpkin had faced danger and adversity before. She was born without a left rear foot. A stray at six weeks old, her right rear leg was cut nearly in half. She limped

94

through the streets and backyards of San Antonio, Texas, eating scraps wherever she could find them, until someone called the Animal Defense League. Rita worked at the no-kill shelter when Pumpkin arrived. "I brought her home to foster her until her severed leg healed," Rita explains. "Watching her determined personality overcome her handicap made us love her even more. With sheer will she taught herself to maneuver through the house and yard on her two front legs, occasionally resting on her left leg, which resembles more of a straight stick. We decided to adopt her ourselves." Pumpkin adjusted nicely to family life and, as it turned out, earned her keep.

By the time the parents, the police, and a neighbor toting a baseball bat arrived at the house, the would-be burglars had fled. There's no doubt the dogs scared them off. It's frightening to consider what might have happened if the intruders stumbled upon Laura and Sara up in the bedroom. "We credit the safety of our children that night to our loyal friends," says Rita.

About a month later, after several more burglaries in the area, two suspects were arrested. Things have since calmed down at the Braeutigam household. The dogs run around together in the backyard, and Pumpkin is unaware of any physical disadvantage. Instead, she's comfortable and secure with a family that's glad to have her.

᷿᷿᷿

Petunia

Pit bulls get a bad rap. People are the ones who turn animals mean; viciousness is not a birthright. Some pit bulls can be the nicest, gentlest pets imaginable, despite their encounters with human cruelty. Take Petunia, for instance.

She was a "bait" dog, deliberately and repeatedly tossed to the wolves, as it were. Violent people used Petunia to taunt and provoke fighting dogs into becoming even more aggressive and then allowed the small, sacrificial youngster to be torn to shreds in order to hone the contestants' skills. This was practice for the real thing: organized dog fights that certain cretins consider a sport.

Somehow on a fall day Petunia managed to escape the torture and was found wandering the streets of Las Vegas, dazed, bloodied and traumatized. Animal control officers picked her up and brought her to the Lied Animal Shelter. Petunia's face and head were ripped open. Her ears dangled by threads. Some of her wounds had been stapled back together, with an office stapler, so that she could be abused some more.

"Little Petunia had been torn apart," says Lied's Janie Gale. But "I've never seen an animal with more heart and soul." Janie, who regularly witnesses things that most folks don't want to think about, was so moved by the sight of the pathetic pit bull with the affectionate eyes that she walked into the hallway and cried. Afterward, they took Petunia to the emergency clinic where her wounds were cleaned and sutured.

A television news reporter learned of the brave little dog and broadcast her story. It was so compelling, other media picked up on Petunia, and soon she became a luminary in a city of stars and lights. Donations arrived, which helped pay for her medical care, including reconstructive surgery. "There was a public outpouring for this sweet little pit," says Janie. Once things settled down, Petunia went to live with a foster family who transformed her from an atrocity survivor to a household pet. But she still needed a permanent home.

As providence would have it, Paula Brown wanted a dog, and she was especially fond of pit bulls. One day between Thanksgiving and Christmas, Paula felt a need to go to the shelter. It was only hours earlier that Petunia's foster mother had returned her to Lied to be put up for adoption. Unaware of Petunia's history, Paula believes "it was truly God leading me to her." When the pair was introduced, Paula sat down on a couch at the shelter, leaned over and their cheeks met. Petunia licked Paula softly on the face. They went home together.

Since her escape, Petunia's life improved with each passing day. She settled into her new home as if she belonged there all along. "She's like an angel dog," says Paula, who takes great comfort from Petunia. "She loves just being wherever you are." Since Paula works from home, they are together all the time. "Petunia is a people dog." Extremely playful and filled with energy, she gets along wonderfully with Paula's husband, the grandchildren, everyone she meets.

Although Petunia bears the physical scars of her past, her emotions withstood the pain and suffering. "She's very forgiving," says Paula. "You wouldn't think she was abused the way she was."

A big heart and a strong will to live guided Petunia through some very dark moments in her early days. A loving family will protect and steer her future. "She's not going to be terrorized ever again," says Janie.

Chloe

Alison and Amie wanted another dog. The little girls loved their old, nearly blind Bernese mountain dog, but she no longer provided much in the way of a romping good time. Mostly she just ate, slept and wagged her tail, dreaming of the days when she was young and full of spirit. By now, though, age had crept up and chased away the puppy inside.

Mom and dad talked about getting another dog who would be more fun for the kids. Although partial to the Bernese breed, they thought it would be nice to visit a shelter and "save a dog's life." After careful consideration buttressed by illogical impulse, dad flew halfway across the country to scout out potential candidates at an animal sanctuary. (It would have made much more sense to drive to a local shelter, but dads aren't always the brightest bulbs in the dog house.)

The sanctuary offered hundreds of dogs to choose from—young, old, purebreds, mutts, everyone a wonderful animal in its own right. That was the dilemma —deciding which dog to adopt. Eventually he entered a pen that housed three little puppies—two brothers and a sister, who were abandoned along with their mother when she gave birth. They jumped all over dad, wagging tiny tails in unison, tugging at his shoelaces, and whining the *boy-are-you-the-neatest-thing-we've-seen-today* greeting. After several minutes of puppy bedlam, the little girl found it hard to keep up with her brothers, so she curled up on a blanket and looked up at dad with sad brown eyes. He watched her, trying to figure out her pedigree. With a tan-and-white coat that sprouted every which way, she looked part cocker spaniel and part dust mop. The puppy saw him staring and lowered her head demurely to outstretched front paws. That did it. "You're the one," dad told her, "let's go home."

As dad strolled through the busy airport toting Chloe in a small container the airline permitted him to carry into the cabin, more than a dozen strangers walked up as her small head popped out the top and looked around in bewilderment. "What a cute, little puppy," each stranger said through a huge smile. "Can I pet it?" Never in a million years would these people have approached an unknown traveler like that, out of the blue, if it weren't for the little dog hanging from his shoulder. Puppies possess a unique ambassadorial quality (along with other qualities) that humans could do well to emulate.

When Chloe and dad arrived at the house late that night, mom greeted them at the door. She whispered "hello" to the tired, frightened puppy, ignored dad, and carried Chloe inside her new home. The kids were asleep, but when they woke up, it was Christmas morning in September. Alison and Amie dashed to greet their new puppy, who scurried for protection under a chair. When the zeal subsided, it was time to think about all the responsibilities involved in raising a pet. More than ten years had gone by since a puppy disrupted their lives.

Mom and dad had forgotten about the joys of housebreaking and the sharp little teeth that can inflict so much damage. In less than a month, Chloe chewed up mom's eyeglasses, dad's wallet, the kids' shoes, a parade of Barbies (with accessories), furniture, everything except her puppy chow. "Why didn't I adopt that friendly, well-trained four-year-old who followed me around the sanctuary," dad thought to himself several times a day as he looked down at spotted carpets.

A few months later, the first snow of the season fell. Watching Chloe chase the flakes with wonder and bound through the tall drifts like a gazelle in quicksand reminded dad why puppies are such fun. Not long afterward, Chloe figured out the bathroom was outdoors and most of the stuff in the house should be chewed only when no one was looking. She became known as the "circus dog" because of her tendency to run through the house at breakneck speed and jump over, on and through the furniture with more agility than most acrobats. Her bottom jaw developed an under-bite, with two lower teeth protruding upward like a vampire in reverse. No matter, that just added to her charm.

From time to time, dad relaxes in the family room recliner and watches the kids playing joyfully with Chloe, realizing that adopting her was indeed a smart move. The Bernese mountain dog lies by his side dreaming of ways to get rid of the pest. Feeling quite satisfied, dad reaches for the TV remote. He can't find it. "Where's the remote?" he asks, although no one in the room is listening. "Has anyone seen the remote? Oh, there it . . . CHLOE!!!"

Sweet Pea

Three sisters ran with abandon along the levee during the early summer, as winter snows melted off the surrounding Tetons of Jackson, Wyoming, and poured into the cold, clear waters of the Snake River. All three girls were once someone's pets, adult mixed-breed dogs who were cast to the perils of the great outdoors, perhaps because two of them carried litters. By necessity they embraced the spirit of the wild, hunting and scavenging for food and keeping their distance from humans.

Often spotted by ranchers, employees of a nearby construction company, and would-be rescuers, the timid animals became local celebrities known as the "levee dogs" or "dike dogs," as they eluded capture along the river and fascinated the mountain community. Be that as it may, when the mothers gave birth the time had come to corral the outcasts for their own good. Animal control officers caught the puppies and two of the three adults and brought them to the Jackson-Teton County Animal Shelter where they were examined, cleaned up and readied for adoption.

One of the mothers became known as Sweet Pea. A gentle but somewhat shy dog with beautiful brown eyes that complemented her thick, black coat and four white paws, Sweet Pea would surely find a permanent home soon, particularly with all the attention the dogs garnered. For some reason, though, that didn't happen. The puppies were adopted, as was her sister. The other mother, who earlier had managed to avoid capture, was finally caught a few months later; and she, too, found a new home. But not Sweet Pea.

As the seasons changed and a new blanket of snow covered the mountains, Sweet Pea waited patiently at the shelter; her thick, black tail with a white tip wagged back and forth like a metronome marking time, as would-be adopters came and went. In February, Alison Brush, a local artist, started thinking about getting a dog and then took the next step. She attended a shelter adoption day and spotted Sweet Pea. "I was immediately struck by how beautiful she was," says Alison. She spent time with the dog and was impressed by her positive attitude. "I left there feeling that this is the dog I want." Alison visited Sweet Pea several more times before making a final decision, recognizing that she was a bit skittish indoors but a true free spirit outdoors. There's no doubt that earlier events helped shape her personality, but it was also clear the abandoned animal had more than enough affection to share if given the chance.

Alison adopted Sweet Pea and took her home to the ranch where she lives. For the first four days, Sweet Pea acted insecure, afraid to do much of anything. Then she changed, one hundred and eighty degrees, overnight. On day five, Sweet Pea opened up as if realizing she was finally safe and partnered with someone who loved her, probably for the first time in her life. "She's been my shadow ever since," says Alison.

Sweet Pea and Alison often go for walks along the river and into the back country, but the dog never strays far from her companion. When asked to sit, she obeys and often embellishes on the command by lifting one paw and then the other, her "high-five and high-ten moves." When she really wants attention, Sweet Pea nudges and kisses Alison, gentle reminders that she's a one-woman dog.

Already a great swimmer, Sweet Pea joined an agility class after several trainers spotted her prowess. "She turns out to be a very athletic and agile dog who won the hearts of her agility trainers," Alison proudly explains. "She is as light as a feather, soaring over any obstacle."

అఎఎ

Tenzing

D r. Tony Casanova named his new rottweiler-German shepherd mix Tenzing after the famous Sherpa, Tenzing Norgay, who together with Edmund Hillary became the first human beings to conquer Mount Everest. More than fifty years after that momentous event, Tony, himself, faces a formidable challenge: he has been diagnosed with multiple sclerosis.

"I thought I should have a good Sherpa in order to get through the gig I'm trying to get through," explains Tony. The debilitating illness forced the successful dentist to give up his practice and it is slowly stealing his mobility. "I used to be an ultra-marathon runner," explains Tony. "Now I get tired when I walk to the refrigerator." It wasn't long ago that Tony also skied the powder off Colorado mountains. He's still a member of the ski patrol, training new patrol members instead of aiding errant snow boarders, but it's slow going along the trails for the former college downhill racer.

Tony adopted the friendly, black-and-brown dog from Colorado Animal Rescue in Glenwood Springs. He, too, has had some rough going. Tenzing lived with a dysfunctional family that abused him until he was taken out of the home by animal control authorities. He was an extra large, lovable and somewhat wild ten-month-old. His manners needed a bit of polishing if he ever wanted to find a new home, so staff members at the shelter went to work on his behavior. After awhile, he was ready to go.

As it turned out, the Colorado State Patrol needed a new working dog, and Tenzing appeared to be an ideal candidate. He performed well, but during the training a veterinarian found a problem in his left rear knee. The physical disability caused him to wash out of class, and he ended up back at the shelter.

At about the same time, Tony decided he needed companionship. "I love dogs and wanted a rottweiler," he remembers. "When I got him, I was so excited." Tony likes the rottweiler's physical appearance as well as its power, intelligence and loving nature.

Tenzing and Tony hit it off right away, but Tenzing's congenital knee problem continued to worsen. He needed all four legs to carry around his nearly one hundred pounds, so Tony decided on surgery. To fix the problem, a veterinarian cut off the dog's leg and then reattached it using a bone graft. Tony was allowed to remain in the operating room throughout the complicated but successful procedure.

Companionship is no longer lacking in the lives of the dentist or the rottweiler-mix. They have each other. They hang around together, look at TV, go for rides, and sleep in the same bedroom. Tenzing is a great watchdog and helps out in other ways around the house, but mostly they just enjoy each other's company. "This boy is living in the lap of luxury," says Tony.

When it is suggested that he did a good thing by giving the dog a new chance, Tony responds: "I think he's saving my life more than I saved his." Although it will be an uphill climb from here on for Tony, he's sure to make the best of it with his partner, Tenzing, by his side.

എഷ

Ben

Ben was like so many other dogs who wind up in shelters throughout the country. He was a stray—probably lived on the streets for years. Before that, the chocolate lab was someone's pet. He was very friendly and obedient—the tail always wagged; he loved men, was great with children, enjoyed fetching and other games. Then one day he was out on the streets, alone. The reason? Unknown.

Ben wandered here and there, scrounged for food and searched for shelter, avoided getting maimed or killed and finally found himself in a kennel at the Oregon Humane Society in Portland. It looked like the end of a hard road for the twelve-year-old. Much of his hair had disappeared, the result of severe mange, and a crop of large, fatty tumors grew in its place. Infection inflamed both ears. Blood pooled in his eyes, perhaps from a fight. At that age and with those health issues, Ben's chances of finding an adoptive home were slim to none.

When shelter volunteer Laura Layton saw Ben for the first time lying on the kennel floor, she thought to herself: put this poor dog out of his misery. But then he "hoisted himself up, came over and started wagging his tail. This dog wants to live," she realized. After looking at him for another moment, she added: "I'll help you." And she did, together with other shelter volunteers. They took it upon themselves to make sure he received appropriate veterinary care and lots of personal attention. "Look into the face of an old dog who has been through a lot. You'll see an incredible will to live," says Laura.

After several months of rehabilitation, the humane society deemed him ready for adoption. Hold on a second, thought Laura, who had become quite fond of Ben and vice versa. If anyone is going to adopt this dog, it's going to be me.

So Ben started a new and far better life. He embarked on his sunset years together with Laura, her cat and other dog, no longer fending for himself alone in the cold and rain. They became a close-knit family, enjoying the security and devotion so easily achieved when humans demonstrate compassion for animals. They played together, traveled and, now and then, did Ben's favorite thing: they headed for the surf. "He loved the beach," Laura says. "He would jump in the ocean, dig in the sand. Many older dogs still love to play, go for walks, ride in cars, swim, play Frisbee and chase squirrels. The upside is they usually tucker out about the same time you do."

Even as time passed, Ben continued to have certain health problems, although they were manageable. And since his hair never grew back completely and he was missing a bunch of teeth, Ben was never mistaken for the peach of the beach. (Some adults thought Ben was rather funny looking. Kids, on the other hand, never seemed to notice his imperfections.) But Ben really didn't care one way or the other. "He had an amazing energy and a real gusto for life," says Laura.

The old, brown Labrador retriever whose chances for survival were once next to nil passed away nearly three years after Laura first met him; they were most likely the best three years of his life. Shortly before he died, Laura threw him a party so that his many friends could come and say goodbye. "He was very happy, even in his last days," she says. "He was a sweet, gentle soul who taught those of us who knew him an appreciation for life. He also taught us to look at dogs differently in terms of who is adoptable."

⸙

Blue

Octogenarian Ruth Gay hooked her family's Australian blue heeler on a leash and took him for a walk in the side yard at about 9 o'clock. It was a warm July night in Fort Myers, Florida, and the grass remained slick from earlier heavy rains that lifted the water in the nearby canal to the top of its banks. During their stroll, Ruth somehow lost her footing and fell hard on the ground, breaking her nose and badly injuring both shoulders. She lay there immobile as the dog named Blue huddled by her side. Ruth yelled for help, although no person would hear; her daughter and son-in-law, Sylvia and Albert Gibson, left the house earlier and would be gone for several hours. Neighboring homes sat deafly in the distance. Ruth and Blue waited alone in the yard . . . until danger joined them.

Out of the darkness, something aroused Blue. He stood up and growled, the fur on the back of his neck pointing toward the great unknown. A moment later he ran off into the night. Ruth couldn't see what was going on but heard a terrible commotion—growling, yelping, whining, bodies rolling around on the lawn. Blue was fighting for his life and, as it turned out, for hers. Suddenly there was silence. Ruth thought Blue died in the struggle. She had no idea what would follow.

Minutes passed slowly, and nothing happened. An hour or more after the fall, Ruth saw her son-in-law rushing in her direction. He carefully helped Ruth to her feet and took her inside. She was covered with ant bites and her shoulders hurt badly. Despite the pain, there was one thing that offered comfort: Blue was alive. The dog had come running up to the Gibson's car when it pulled in the driveway. He was soaking wet, wearing his leash, and "barking and carrying on," remembers Sylvia. It became clear something was wrong as Blue led them to the fallen grandmother. While preparing to take Ruth to the hospital, they noticed blood on the floor. It wasn't Ruth's and it didn't appear to be coming from Blue.

It was early in the morning when Albert finally left the hospital and headed home to check on Blue, the young dog that he adopted for his grandson when the dog's original owners gave him away for free because they considered him a handful. Blue heelers are known to be smart, loyal, protective and always at the center of the action. "He's his own dog," says Sylvia. "Blue likes things to go right and lets people know if something is out of order."

Something was definitely wrong when Albert got home: the dog didn't move. He examined Blue closely and discovered deep puncture wounds, some thirty in all. Blue's battle several hours earlier had been with an alligator, most likely one of the six- to twelve-footers sighted in the canal. Astonishingly, the dog lived to wag another day. The alligator survived as well, spotted not long afterward nursing some nasty bite wounds of its own.

At two o'clock in the afternoon both Ruth and Blue were rolled into surgery in their respective medical facilities. Ruth remained in the hospital for six weeks and then continued her recovery at home. Blue healed quicker with the help of antibiotics and waited to greet Ruth when she arrived at the house. He often stayed in her room during the convalescence, just to make sure everything was okay. "He worries about all of us," says Sylvia.

Word of Blue's heroism spread far and wide. Had Blue not intervened when Ruth lay injured in the yard, there's little doubt the alligator would have killed her. Newspapers, magazines and television stations recounted the story. Awards were bestowed on the brave two-year-old, including the title of grand marshal at a parade in California.

No one will ever know what went through Blue's mind that night, staring eyeball-to-eyeball with an alligator, realizing that it was up to him to protect a loved one. Wrestling alligators is not for the faint of heart. Maybe he is a handful, but don't expect him to be given away any time soon.

Alvin

When the rescuer from the Humane Society of Pulaski County stopped her vehicle on the shoulder of the road one weekday morning, she was moments away from witnessing a remarkable act of tenderness. Four or five motorists called the shelter to report a black dog lying in a pile of leaves on the side of an Arkansas roadway. It was winter and especially cold. If the dog had been hit by a car in the dark of night, the odds that it survived to see the sunrise were slim. Nonetheless, Kay Jordan of the humane society asked the rescuer to drive to the scene to see if anything could be done.

As she approached the body, she noticed movement. It was still alive. The tail of the stocky chow-German shepherd mix wagged as if to say: *glad to see you*. Then Alvin slowly started to rise, revealing his true purpose for being there. Beneath the big black dog lay a small brown dog who was bleeding and badly injured.

The pair were friends and had roamed the streets together, sharing food and water, covering each other's tail. Sometime in the night a car thundered by and struck the smaller dog. She managed to crawl to the side of the road before collapsing into the dead leaves. Uninjured himself, Alvin hurried to his companion's side and then selflessly spread his body across hers to protect her from the cold and dangers of the night. They remained huddled together until help arrived.

Alvin gratefully allowed the rescuer to pick up his friend and carry her to the emergency vehicle. "There was no aggressiveness, no growling, nothing," says Kay. Alvin hopped in beside her, and they headed for the veterinarian's office. The angelic, wounded stray captured everyone's heart. "She was really sweet." They tried their best to save her, but the injuries were too extensive, and she died during surgery.

Although she didn't make it, her final hours might have been much worse. The little brown dog could have easily frozen to death alone at the side of the road. Instead, Alvin draped her with love until caring humans arrived to ease her pain and offer more compassion than she may have ever known in her lifetime. There was comfort in the end.

As for Alvin, they cleaned him up at the humane society, and a few days later he appeared on local television. His story touched viewers' hearts. "Immediately, the phone started ringing," says Kay. People wanted to find out how he was doing and how they could help. Within two weeks, Alvin was adopted by an emergency services worker who brought the three-year-old home to join his family. "They feel lucky to have him," Kay reports.

No wonder. He's a great dog: smart, friendly gentle, "a big baby." At one point in his life, Alvin was someone else's pet, but they never bothered to look for him when he went missing. These days Alvin plays ball, goes fishing and loves to ride in the front seat of the pickup truck. He's grown especially close to one family member who is quite ill.

And then there are the grandchildren. When they play outside, Alvin always keeps them in sight. He never lets them get too close to the street.

Jeddy

The little lost dog meandered around the huge parking lot at a mass merchandise store searching for something to do. Hungry, dirty and all alone, he needed a little food and attention, not to mention a bath. Two young boys rode up on bicycles and played with him for awhile, but soon they had to go home, so they walked into the store and told a customer service employee about the friendly stray outside. Coincidentally, an animal rescuer was standing within earshot, and the eighteen-month-old Tibetan spaniel's misfortunes were about to change.

"He was very, very dirty and wearing a black harness with no identification tag," explains Samantha Pettingill of the Society for Pet Adoption, Rescue and Education (SPARE) in Bear, Delaware. Her mother, Julie, was the woman waiting at the customer service desk when the boys came in. Samantha and Julie were on their way to deliver a dog who had just been adopted from SPARE when they stopped for a moment at the store. Since that dog was leaving, it seemed reasonable to take in another.

They scooped up their new friend, who was later named Jeddy, turned around and headed for home to drop him off before continuing on with their original mission.

Jeddy loved the brief ride; he sat on a comfortable lap and gazed out the window as the lonely world he endured passed by and a new life that included warmth and kindness emerged.

Samantha is not sure if Jeddy was abandoned on purpose or simply wandered off without anyone caring if he returned. SPARE placed lost dog advertisements and contacted appropriate authorities, but the owner never responded. Jeddy's original family "probably wanted him when they first got him and just ignored him after that," Samantha suspects. "He was just there, part of the furniture. I don't think he had ever been bathed." When Samantha washed the caked-on crud from his skinny body, she discovered a beautiful white coat with tan markings. He was a handsome little guy . . . great disposition, too. Always happy and exuberant, "he was a very good dog," says Samantha, "a fun dog to be around. He made you smile." A die-hard couch potato, Jeddy loved to jump into Samantha's lap, flip over on his back and hope for a belly rub.

When Jeddy was ready, Samantha showed him off at several adoption events and posted his photo on an Internet adoption site. Several people expressed interest, but Samantha turned them down. She and Julie wanted just the right home for Jeddy. A few months later, a woman from Pennsylvania who saw Jeddy on the Web called to learn more. She was a receptionist at a veterinarian's office, had two cats and wanted a small dog. This was the match they were looking for. Jeddy soon moved to a nice house in the suburbs, albeit to the temporary dismay of the two cats, but that sorted itself out quickly. Now he spruces up and volunteers as a therapy dog at hospitals and nursing homes; no longer lost and alone, instead surrounded by people who are glad he's around.

❦

The Madcap Mutts

As the troupe of performing dogs endowed with mixed lineage takes a breather on stage, their trainer and fellow entertainer, Tom Brackney, looks out at the charmed audience and asks: "Remember when your children were really little, and they were teething, and they were cranky, and they cried all the time? You didn't give your kids away, did you? . . . You thought about it, but you didn't."

The message is serious although it's delivered amid a lively exhibition of agility, obedience and tail-wagging merriment. Tom and his wife, Bonnie, created the Madcap Mutts show several decades ago. Their mission "is to raise awareness of the numbers of dogs and cats available for adoption at shelters and humane societies across the United States; to educate the public as to the importance of spaying and neutering; and to help shelters raise money to deal with the ongoing problem of unwanted dogs and cats."

They accomplish their objectives with a small gang of "second-hand mutts" who were tossed aside by their original families. Obviously, those folks didn't recognize talent when they saw it.

There's Marty, a "handsome hunk with big, soft eyes" whose owners surrendered him to a New York City shelter because he chewed too much. Since then, he has starred on Broadway and in TV commercials. "It turns out they gave away a really smart dog," says Tom. Susie was abandoned and found refuge in a Missouri barn. Feminine and sweet, but "built like a small Mack truck," she loves to cradle in Tom's arms and sing to anyone who will listen. Stormy hails from Philadelphia, where he caused his original owner's allergies to flare up. With enough energy to fuel a squadron of eagles, Stormy walks on his hind legs, barks on cue and steals Tom's hat during the act. Minnie used to make her home in Minneapolis until she was thrown out for jumping on the furniture. She invented her own trick one day during a performance by bouncing up and down in a barrel, not on cue. The audience loved it.

Scooter is "the sweetest dog we have ever known," say Tom and Bonnie. They can't imagine why someone would have pulled to the side of the road in rural northern New Jersey, not far from the Madcap Mutts' home base, and kicked him out of the car. Yet he still offers a kiss and a wag to everyone he meets—that is, when he is not balancing on a suspended rope in front of hundreds of people. Sandy suffered physical abuse before landing in a shelter in Port Jervis, New York. "She is living proof that just about any second-hand pet can be returned to a normal life as a faithful companion," say Tom and Bonnie. "She has become a valuable addition to the show."

Holly, aka "The Mutt That Kicks Butt," pummels Tom's posterior when he turns his back on her during the show. She, too, was abandoned in the Garden State. Evidently she doesn't want a loved one to turn away from her ever again. In this case it is doubtful; Holly sleeps at night in the Brackney's bedroom. Rusty's career began on the other side of the Pond, when Tom and Bonnie adopted him from a shelter in Germany. At the time, they were members of *Holiday on Ice* touring through Europe. Tom was a professional skater who incorporated dogs into his routines. Bonnie's family started a dog and pony show in 1939, and performances have continued ever since, in one fashion or another. Their complementary expertise gave birth to the Madcap Mutts. Rusty returned to the States with Tom and Bonnie, and now he reminds children to say no to smoking and drugs.

There's bound to be one in every group of celebrities, and Sally's the one: a "high-maintenance blonde" who seems to care more about her hair than anything else. She was abandoned in Las Vegas. That could explain it. Pepper came from Detroit with enough pep to drive a motor vehicle piston, too much for her original owner. The energy, however, has been channeled into a positive force in the act. "Once airborne, her hang time rivals that of Michael Jordan going to the hoop," say her trainers. Amos was a small abandoned puppy when he was rescued and raised by the Brackneys. He's still working on his confidence, but in terms of agility, Amos is right on the mark.

By now, some readers may have recognized the mutts. They performed for several years in the original Broadway production of *The Will Rogers Follies*, toured with *Holiday on Ice*, appeared in television shows and commercials, strutted their stuff at Radio City Music Hall and at other venues throughout the world. It's been a long grind, but the benefits are many.

Discussing her beloved pets, some of whom have retired, Bonnie explains: "They were surrendered because of behavioral problems. It doesn't take very long to turn that bad habit into a productive one." If only kids were that easy.

Misha

While church organists rehearsed joyous holiday music and shoppers scurried about in search of last-minute presents, Rick and Susan Rude of McLean, Virginia, chose Christmas Eve to give the gift of kindness to a tiny, very sick puppy who needed a miracle to live to see her first birthday.

The solid white coton de tulear weighed less than four pounds when the Washington Animal Rescue League picked her up a few days earlier from a breeder who kept the starving animal locked in a bird cage in a dark cellar and fed her kitty litter to keep her quiet. The breeder knew there was little chance of selling the dog who, if healthy, could fetch a hefty price, because she was seriously ill. So the dog just wasted away in the cage, lying in her own urine and feces, until someone alerted authorities. "They just put her in there to die," says Rick. "Her chances of survival were virtually nil."

Rescuers took the anxious, helpless puppy, later named Misha, to a veterinary hospital where doctors determined her heart was defective, but the exact nature of the illness could be determined only through extensive testing. Shelter workers fed Misha as much real food as she could handle, cleaned her up and then crossed their fingers. Coincidentally, or perhaps inexplicably, Rick contacted the shelter at the same time to make a contribution. Earlier in the year he and Susan adopted a coton de tulear and a silky terrier mix from the shelter and wanted to express their gratitude. During their conversation, the league's executive director told Rick about Misha, a frightened little dog who probably didn't have much time to live. Rick and Susan agreed the sweet, mistreated animal deserved the opportunity to experience comfort and love, even if only for a short time. "We'll take care of her for as long as she needs care," he thought. "This is something my wife and I feel we should do."

The day before Christmas, Rick and Susan adopted Misha and took her directly to their own veterinarian, who stayed open longer than planned to help out. The examination results stifled the season's merriment. "We expected her to die any day," says Rick. Nonetheless, they decided to make an appointment with a cardiologist to see if something more could be done. In the interim, Susan and Rick took the frail puppy home and fed her tiny portions of special food with a small spoon to try to keep her alive until the specialist could see her. The cardiologist found that one of the valves in Misha's heart was obstructed; what's more, there was a hole in her heart. The only chance she had, and it was a long shot, involved complicated surgery. "The heart was becoming massively enlarged," explains Rick. The cardiologist referred Susan and Rick to the Virginia-Maryland Regional College of Veterinary Medicine, one of the few institutions in the country with the equipment and expertise to perform the surgery.

By this time, many people might have given up; the odds were against them, not to mention the bills that piled up. Susan and Rick already had three other dogs and a cat. Why go any further? "It was the right thing to do," explains Rick. "We're (humans) the protectors of animals on this planet. They give us a lot more than they take."

In early February, after Misha grew strong enough to attempt surgery, she went under the knife in an effort to correct the obstructed valve. It was a delicate, sophisticated operation, using procedures similar to those that doctors employ on babies . . . and it worked. The surgery went so well, "it was almost textbook," says Rick. Next, the hole in Misha's heart needed to be closed. A month later, Misha went in for her second surgery. That, too, proved successful. "She is now about as fixed as humanly possible," says Rick, who gratefully acknowledges that all of the people involved with Misha's care went out of their way to help her.

Today, Misha is healthy and looking forward to a long and happy life. "She's a survivor," says Rick. "This dog has been an absolute gift." Misha's doggy pals, Fifi, Lila and Angel, make sure she doesn't overdo it as they play together at home. "They get along very well," says Rick. As for the cat? "She sits on top of the dining room table and watches all of them with a great deal of disdain." It's unclear as to how many more Christmas miracles Kitty can handle.

Avery

*I*ch bin ein lucky puppy. He's no German shepherd, but Avery's ear for the language may have saved his life.

It all began on a lovely spring day when a sheriff's deputy found the young, brown-and-white hound mix lying injured at the side of an Alabama highway. The officer stopped his vehicle, carefully picked up the fifty-pound dog, and then drove to the Tuscaloosa Metro Animal Shelter. When the deputy and his patient arrived and the animal's chances for survival were assessed, they didn't look promising.

"The dog appeared to be in shock and unresponsive to our voices," explains Judy Hill. "Our shelter handles over 7,000 animals a year and, with no veterinarian on staff, it is my call as director to decide if any animal should be sent to a veterinarian for treatment. Just as I was beginning to lean toward euthanasia, because of its condition and the fact that it had no I.D. or microchip, one of our volunteers approached the deputy's truck and started talking to the dog."

Volunteer Petra Jonas, originally from Germany, leaned close to the traumatized dog and spoke softly and reassuringly in her native tongue. What happened next surprised everyone. "He lifted his head slightly and started wagging his tail," says Judy. "I just stood there in amazement and could not believe what a difference she made in the dog's struggle to live." Perhaps Avery understood German, or maybe it was Petra's special way with animals. No one will ever know for sure, but the dog's response to her soothing voice caused Judy to reevaluate the situation.

She decided to send Avery to the vet to see if there was a chance he might make it. The exam uncovered a few minor injuries, but he was basically in good shape, considering he had just been hit by a car and left to die at the side of a road. After a few days of rest and recuperation, Avery headed back to the shelter. The affectionate, possibly bilingual one-year-old now needed a home.

Avery, who was named after the veterinarian who helped him convalesce, wiggled his way into the hearts of the shelter employees and volunteers. "He was a sweet, sweet dog with a great personality," says Judy. "I can't image why no one came forward to claim him, although that happens all the time."

Judy believes it was Avery's personality that attracted the paramedic who came to the shelter to adopt a pet a few months later. The pair hit it off, and the man took Avery home. Today, Avery lives the comfortable life of a well-cared-for family pet. He "is a true testament to the spirit that a dog possess," says Judy. For Avery, the wurst is over.

❧

Duke

People who devote their lives to helping abandoned and abused animals witness human cruelty on a regular basis. But for Lorraine Jackson, founder of the Adopt-A-Pet no-kill shelter in Benld, Illinois, this brutal act was more horrific than she could imagine.

Lorraine was called to a local veterinarian's office one hot summer day to take a look at an extremely thin, white German shepherd mix that was brought in by police more dead than alive. "There were huge patches of hair and flesh torn from him. His feet were almost four times their usual size," Lorraine remembers. "Half of his face was torn badly. The rim of his eye was fractured and the flesh torn away. He had a huge open hole in the top of his head. But his beautiful brown eyes were open, and he looked up at me and wagged his tail in greeting."

What happened to the one-year-old family pet should be the stuff of morbid fiction, but it is not. Duke was tied to the back of a pickup truck and dragged down the road for two miles, while the driver's children pleaded with their father to stop the vehicle. They knew their pet was tumbling and scraping in agony along the pavement. Witnesses saw the atrocity as well and called police. The driver told authorities he did not remember the dog was attached to the bumper. They arrested him, nonetheless, for cruelty to an animal. He was never prosecuted but did agree to relinquish the dog to Lorraine.

"The doctor thought there was no hope for the dog," says Lorraine. "But the dog didn't die. He fought to live, and the doctor knew it would take a miracle to help him survive."

It also took months of loving care from Lorraine to nurse him back to health. She brought Duke home, placed him on a soft bed and connected an intravenous bottle that dripped life into his veins. It was like treating a burn victim. Every day she lifted him gently into a tub of warm water, used a wire brush to remove the dead, abraded skin and then cleaned his wounds.

"He was the best patient anyone could ask for," says Lorraine. "Through all the agony of the necessary treatments, Duke never once acted aggressively." Instead, he sometimes looked up at Lorraine lovingly and kissed her, as if to say: *I know you're trying to help.*

"Ever so slowly, his wounds began to heal," says Lorraine. "He walked alone. Most of his hair returned. A veterinarian grafted muscle to create another eyelid. The hole in the top of his head closed, and he knew love from gentle hands and soft words. Here was a dog who knew nothing but hunger, cruelty and horrible abuse in his young life, but he didn't let the past affect his future."

Indeed, his destiny began to follow a dramatic new course. People heard about Duke's plight and donated money to help pay for the medical expenses. When he was physically able, Lorraine began taking him on mobile adoptions to meet supporters and well-wishers. He handled each new situation with courage and friendliness, always offering a wag of the tail to strangers who stopped to say hello. "The dog loves everybody," Lorraine admits.

In time, he became Adopt–A–Pet's official mascot, visiting schools, nursing homes, and attending special events, helping to educate the public and adding a little joy to the lives of others. "He's our goodwill ambassador," says Lorraine.

Duke overcame tremendous odds. Permanent scars will always traverse his body, reminders of dreadful physical abuse, but his spirit is another story. It remains unscathed and vibrant.

Dudley

The nine-year-old boy looked forward to getting a dog for a long time. Martin wanted a trusted companion and, more importantly, he needed one to help with daily activities, like turning on a light or getting a drink from the refrigerator. Muscular dystrophy prevented the youngster from doing many of the things most kids his age took for granted . . . until he met Dudley.

The big German shepherd mix is a service dog, specially trained by Hawaii Canines for Independence (HCI) to provide his partner with the freedom and confidence to lead a more independent life. Dudley and Martin, who is confined to a motorized wheelchair, mastered their objective in no time at all. "The payoff is so immense," says the boy's mother, "we're very grateful."

Destiny brought the boy and his dog together. A year and a half earlier, Dudley's future seemed less than promising. As a very young puppy, he and his litter-mates were picked up as strays on the streets of Haiku and taken to the Maui Humane Society. Dudley acted darling, as do all puppies, but he appeared to be rather ordinary.

Then one day, Mo Maurer of HCI stopped by the humane society shelter. She saw a special spark in Dudley's eye. "There was something about him," she explains.

Soon afterward, Dudley found himself enrolled in service dog training. First he went to live with a volunteer puppy-raiser family. He stayed with them for almost a year, learning socialization skills and basic obedience. He really hit it off with a boy in the family, a precursor for his upcoming pairing.

From there he moved on to advanced training at HCI, where he learned some ninety different commands through positive reinforcement and behavior modification. When he mastered the necessary skills, Dudley met Martin. They underwent psychological, physical and emotional tests, and trained together to make sure they functioned well as a team. No problem.

"He's hilarious," Martin says, referring to Dudley, who is known to lavish kisses upon anyone who will accept them. "He can get my parents when it rains and they can't hear me, and he can pick up everything I drop." The dog also pulls up the boy's blankets in the middle of the night when it gets cold, helps find lost items, opens doors—literally and figuratively, and much, much more. Perhaps most importantly, he's a best friend.

That litter of puppies (all have been adopted) that was tossed away like yesterday's trash produced a talented and faithful companion who enriches the life of a deserving child. As it turns out, there's nothing ordinary about Dudley.

Ghost & Princess

The eccentric, middle-aged stranger rolled into the rural Maine town one day in his RV, accompanied by twenty-seven dogs. His name was John, and they say he drove up from Florida to settle on a piece of land he owned in the woods. It's a mystery as to where the dogs came from, let alone how they all fit into the RV.

When they arrived, John parked his vehicle on his land, erected a fifty-foot-by-fifty-foot fence and hunkered down for those cold nights in northern New England. The RV served as home; the only shelter for the dogs was the cap of an old truck. John loved his dogs but he couldn't afford them. Several kindhearted people donated food, and John sometimes did without himself in order to make sure his dogs were fed, but there wasn't much left for necessities, like adequate shelter and medical care. Good intentions come at a price.

In time, people in town grew concerned for the animals' welfare. John tended to his large pack of mixed breeds as well as he knew how and gave some of them away to townsfolk, but nearly two dozen dogs remained. As winter approached, one caring neighbor contacted several shelters, including Paws Humane Society of Calais, a small, no-kill shelter about an hour and a half away. Although Paws was filled, Robin Dufour said she would help out. John agreed to let some of the dogs go, and ten of them traveled to Paws.

"There's no way I was going to refuse those dogs," says Robin. "They needed help, and they needed it big time. We were very concerned, because those dogs had no shelter." The animals were not hungry, but they were dirty and frightened, and several required medical attention. Five of the dogs arrived with porcupine quills embedded in their skin; surgery was required to remove some of the sharp spines. One dog died of pneumonia. However, for the most part they were well, very timid and nervous, but physically okay. It would take awhile, though, to gain their trust. "These dogs really needed time and love."

They received both at Paws. Robin and others at the shelter employed a strategy of ham and turkey entice-ments to get the dogs to warm up to strangers. Eventu-ally, each animal came around. "Once you have its trust, you have a wonderful dog," explains Robin. Soon the dogs were ready for adoption, and six of them found new homes. Ghost and Princess are two of the remaining dogs. They are young Akita-shepherd mixes, with light-colored hair and tails that curl up over their backs. Robin be-lieves that Ghost is the mother of Princess, but there's no way to be sure. "These are our babies. They'll be here for as long as it takes," says Robin, who will only adopt them out as a pair. They eat together, sleep together, play to-gether, and stand by one another. There's no way they'll be separated. "I think they need one another."

Nearly a year after Paws took in the dogs, the shelter learned of a tragic ending to John's unusual story. A kerosene heater in his RV caught fire one night, and John died in the blaze. Several of his dogs still remained in the pen, unhurt by the fire, but they were later put down by authorities.

Ghost, Princess, and the other rescued dogs live on, however. It remains a mystery as to where they came from or what their destiny might have been were it not for the man who charted his own peculiar course and the benevolent animal lovers who helped save most of his passengers when the going got too rough.

Lucky D

There's good luck and there's bad luck. This black Labrador retriever-mix tasted more than his share of both.

Appropriately named Lucky D (D is for dog), he started out with the bad variety. Fulton County Animal Control officers rescued the six-month-old from a miserable, neglectful existence. When they picked him up, Lucky D suffered from a severely ingrown collar. His owner never bothered to replace the collar as the dog developed, so the puppy's skin grew over the two-inch-wide strap, much like tree bark enveloping a guide wire. Unfortunately, this is not an uncommon form of abuse. When the facts were presented to the court, Lucky D's owner was sentenced to forty hours of community service for animal neglect.

The retriever's luck started to change for the better when he arrived at the clinic of the Atlanta Humane Society (AHS). He spent seventeen days recovering from the neck wound and, just when he started feeling fit and ready for adoption, Lucky D came down with a nasty case of mange due to his weakened condition and the stress he previously suffered. The not-so-Lucky D landed back in the clinic for twelve weeks of isolation and recovery.

"Thinking his problems were over, Lucky, now too big for the puppy room, moved into the big dog room in hopes of finding a family," reports Katherine Christenson of the AHS. "To make him even more attractive to the public, Lucky was enrolled in the AHS Manners Matters program and managed to further wiggle his way into the hearts of staff and volunteers." The program teaches dogs basic obedience, which can often improve their chances for adoption.

Six months after he was rescued, Lucky D was adopted. Good luck seemed to be rolling his way . . . briefly. On the first day he arrived at his new home, experiencing the joy and exuberance of a fresh start at life, Lucky D charged through a plate glass window. Back he went to the AHS clinic to staple shut the wound in his chest and for ten more days of recovery. The new owner decided the fit wasn't right, so Lucky D was up for adoption once again.

Staffers at the AHS began to wonder if there was any hope for this happy, friendly young dog who couldn't seem to catch a break. Everyone there loved him. They tried their best to find him a home, but time and circumstance worked against him. In what might have been a final attempt at adoption, Katherine appeared on a local television news program with Lucky D, pleading for a good family to take him and explaining the dangers of ingrown collars.

"A wonderful couple saw Lucky and fell in love immediately," explains Katherine. "Two days later, Lucky was adopted and finally found a permanent, loving family. He now lives on two acres, loves to play ball and is living the luxurious life of an only child." On any given day he can be observed snuggling comfortably on his own little couch watching cartoons on TV.

Fortune occasionally favors the innocent. Less than one year after thoughtlessness nearly suffocated the unlucky puppy, he found himself leading the pack as grand marshal of the Twelfth Annual Atlanta Humane Society Pet Parade at Six Flags Over Georgia. The honored guest took it all in stride.

∽✦∾

Butch

(South Carolina)

When Butch arrived at the Frances R. Willis SPCA shelter in South Carolina on a cool November day, both he and his prospects looked grim. "You could see every rib in his body," explains Ben Black, executive director of the facility. Thanks to a nasty case of mange and the miserable life he had led up until that point, Butch "had no hair on his body, except a little bit on his head and paws. He had open sores all over his back and sides. Ticks were feeding off his sores. He was also dehydrated and covered with fleas." Despite his physical condition, the boxer-mastiff mix was a friendly young guy, not shy or frightened by the strangers. "He was very excited to be taken away from the life he was in," says Ben. Many dogs who come from bad situations are grateful to be rescued from harm's way. They seem to sense the mistreatment is over.

In terms of abuse, Butch had been chained to the rearview mirror of a beat-up pickup truck that was languishing in his owner's backyard. Although there was a doghouse near the truck that could have protected the one-year-old from the heat, cold and nasty weather, the chain didn't reach far enough. So the dog remained chained outdoors without shelter and given very little food or water. The owner certainly could have connected a longer chain or moved the house to within reach of the poor dog, but he didn't. Ben believes it was a deliberate act of cruelty.

The animal control officer cited the owner twice, demanding the dog be provided with proper living conditions. That didn't happen, so on the third visit the officer took Butch away from his foul existence and brought him to the shelter. SPCA staff members took one look at him and agreed his days were numbered. In most instances, no one wants to adopt an animal in that condition and it is eventually euthanized.

After a medical check-up, Butch was placed in a holding pen that happened to be right outside the executive director's office. Ben saw Butch quite often. "He always had a big smile on his face," Ben remembers, and always ran exuberantly around in circles whenever Ben came near. "He touched my heart. For a dog that had been through so much in the early stages of his life, he had such a happy attitude."

After a few days, Ben started taking Butch into his office, where he curled up into a ball and fell fast asleep. At home one night Ben told his wife, Paige, also an animal lover, that he would like to adopt Ben. "I can assure you, it wasn't for his looks," Ben admits. Based on what Paige heard about the dog, it didn't seem like such a great idea. But she decided to go meet Butch anyway. Ben remembers when Paige first saw him: "Her mouth just about hit the floor." Tears welled up in her eyes. The poor dog—it was obvious that he had a wonderful personality, but what a challenge it would be to address his physical needs. And there could be other things wrong that were still undetected. After a few minutes of consideration, "she decided to give it a shot."

It took several months of extremely painful treatment for his sores to heal and brindled coat to grow back. But Butch recovered nicely. He put on about twenty-five pounds and is "excited to be alive," according to Ben. "He's as fat and happy a dog as you've ever seen."

Butch goes to work daily with Ben, plays with dogs at the shelter, and sleeps in the office across from his old holding pen, where he once awaited the strong possibility of a premature death.

"You can find a diamond in the rough at an SPCA," Ben says. Butch turned out so well, people regularly inquire as to how they can adopt him. One person asked to buy him. "If in exchange for Butch you gave me a suitcase with a million dollars in it, I wouldn't take it. The joy he brings to my wife and me, you can't put a price on it."

Jesse

Jesse sniffed intently and moved gingerly through piles of twisted metal and dust-covered debris as she searched for evidence that would ultimately bring some measure of finality to grief-stricken loved ones. Suddenly the yellow lab stopped and signaled to Lisa that she found something: the partial remains of a person who walked into the Pentagon on a beautiful sunny morning but never walked out.

"Like most Americans on September 11, 2001, I watched the events unfolding on television and wished I could help," explains Lisa Nyland, a corporal with the Maryland Natural Resource Police. "The opportunity came sooner than expected." A little more than a week later, the K-9 handler and her cadaver dog were asked to help locate the remains of the victims of the devastating terrorist attack. They, along with some thirty other K-9 teams, worked in the "hot zone," searching inch by inch through piles of building fragments, shattered office equipment and mangled personal effects in an effort to find and identify those who died there. They probed for twenty to thirty minutes at a stretch, stopped to be decontaminated and rest briefly, and then continued searching for evidence. Jesse and Lisa served at the

143

Pentagon for six days. "Because of the dogs, 185 of 189 victims were identified. That wouldn't have been possible without the dogs," says Lisa. She hopes their efforts brought some comfort to the families of the victims.

Like many other dogs who perform valuable services for mankind, Jesse hails from the ranks of the unwanted. The friendly eight-month-old stray appeared from nowhere one day and hung around a mobile home park, devouring bits and pieces of food a kindhearted person tossed her way. After a few weeks, someone called animal control authorities and Jesse landed in the Caroline County (Maryland) Animal Shelter. That turned out to be her big break. Lisa happened to be looking for a dog to train for search and rescue and heard about the "super intelligent, outgoing but not aggressive" yellow lab at the shelter. "Her personality instantly appealed to me," says Lisa. They went home together the evening they met.

Lisa and Jesse learned the ins and outs of search, rescue, recovery, and cadaver detection when they joined the East Coast K-9 Search and Rescue organization. Aside from the Pentagon, their most famous recovery occurred five years earlier when a teenage mother and father discarded their newborn baby in Delaware. Police suspected the cadaver might have been deposited in a dumpster behind a hotel, and they called in Jesse to investigate. The dog immediately detected something in the right, bottom of the trash container. "I climbed into the dumpster and recovered the body of a newborn in a plastic bag," says Lisa. None too soon—as it turned out, while Lisa was inside the container, trash collectors were next door. Their next stop was the hotel dumpster.

"Without Jesse's help, the infant may have never been recovered."

Another grizzly assignment involved the conviction of a guy who killed a man, chopped him into pieces, stuffed the remains in the trunk of a car, and then dumped the victim in another state. The suspect was later stopped by police and the car impounded. Jesse detected a foul scent in the trunk. Her efforts helped send the murderer to prison for life.

There was a happier ending to another of Jesse's missions when on a July 4th weekend she saved a thirteen-year-old boy scout who wandered away from his camp and became lost in thick woods for two days. Jesse found the frightened, but otherwise healthy, scout and stayed by him until help arrived.

Since they began as a team, Lisa and Jesse have searched for drowning victims, suicides, missing children, nursing home walk-offs, dementia patients, lost hunters, even a lost dog. They've helped the FBI as well as police agencies and fire departments in Maryland, Delaware, Pennsylvania and New Jersey.

"I'll have many dogs in my life, but none can be as special as her," says Lisa. "She's my heart. She's taught me more about patience, persistence and canine behavior than I'll ever learn from any one else . . . a truly extraordinary dog."

❧

Romeo

He nearly ended up like a Shakespearian tragedy but, fortunately, this Romeo will have to wait for his everlasting rest. Alas, just three years old, innocent and full of life, the friendly collie-mix was scheduled to die on a fine July day in North Dakota. Romeo's time ran out at the pound, but a reprieve came at the eleventh hour when the Pet Connection Humane Society in Bismarck decided to rescue the dog and offer him another chance.

The sixty-pound stray, who at one time was someone's pet, immediately garnered the affections of the shelter staff. "He has a very nice, calm temperament," says Barb Plum of the Pet Connection. He's also very smart, smart enough to endear himself to everyone he meets. In fact, Romeo was such a lover, he spent most of his time in the front-end of the facility, greeting guests, volunteers and employees.

But that wasn't his true calling. Romeo was born to be a therapy dog; his instincts, his demeanor, everything about the intelligent, gentle mongrel suggested that his mission in life was to bring happiness to people who needed it. Barb acknowledges that "he had a job to do."

Romeo turned out to be a natural for the Pet Connection's therapy dog program. He visited nursing homes, hospitals and other institutions, standing calmly beside beds and wheelchairs as patients stroked his golden-brown and black coat and whispered sentimental secrets into his attentive ears. They told him about their pets at home, how they missed them, and how much joy he brought to them at that very moment.

Romeo loved his job, loved his new friends, and they reciprocated. Once, though, a dark moment overcame an old man suffering from dementia; one minute he gently stroked the dog, the next he kicked him hard in the side. Even the best of animals might have retaliated. Romeo did not. He dropped to the floor and looked perplexedly at his handler. That was it.

After living and working at the Pet Connection for two years, and occasionally playing mother hen to baby kittens who awaited new homes, Romeo was adopted by a former employee who had spent a great deal of time with him. Soon thereafter, one of the institutions Romeo visited asked if he could come to live with them as the resident therapy dog. His owner agreed, and Romeo landed a permanent, full-time position, doing what he was born to do. The abandoned stray who was once only hours away from death now brings "so much joy to so many people," says Barb.

Thus, with a kiss, and lots of hugs and caresses, Romeo lives.

Bralie

S he never saw them coming, but she could hear their voices. The old, blind German shepherd mix with tumors sprouting across her body sat alone in the shelter and waited. She checked in several weeks earlier and was earmarked a stray. The chances of Bralie ever being adopted were as remote as her vision; people rarely offer second chances to dogs in her condition. Her date with demise was overdue, and the voices she heard coming closer could well be the last she would ever hear. It would take a miracle to save the sweet old girl who loved to wag her tail and lick the faces of those who paid her even the slightest attention.

But when the kennel door opened and they leashed the sorrowful-looking dog, she sidestepped the path to euthanasia and, instead, headed out the front door toward the safe and loving home of Lila Hemenway-Terrell, founder of Noah's Bark Pet Rescue. "The thought of her just haunted me," says Lila, who visited the shelter reluctantly that morning, not intending to rescue another animal. She already had four older dogs, one of them blind. Even with her rescue plate full, Lila thought to herself: "I can't leave her. The minute I leave this shelter, she is going to be put to sleep."

On the way home that day in late July, Lila asked herself: "What the heck am I going to do with a ten-year-old, blind, tumor-infested dog? How am I going to find her a home?" Noah's Bark is a group that rescues animals in Southern California. Volunteers care for the animals in their own homes until the pets are adopted. Sometimes, they remain there for life. The next day, Lila took Bralie to the vet, who spayed her and removed the tumors. Afterward, she returned home to join the other dogs. "They sort of moved over on the sofa and made room for her," says Lila.

Bralie adapted well to her new surroundings. She quickly figured out how to walk through the house without bumping into things, became very attached to Lila, and enjoyed the company of her canine buddies. Because the dog was so friendly, trusting of people and not hand-shy (some blind dogs are when touched), Lila had a hard time believing Bralie was a stray. "She seemed like she belonged to a family," says Lila, who placed "found" ads in the newspaper to see if her owner would come forward. Nonetheless, after three months it looked as though Bralie had settled into her permanent home.

Then one morning in October, the same friend who convinced Lila to go to the shelter the day she adopted Bralie suggested that they and the dogs attend a pet adoption street fair in a nearby town. Maybe one of the dogs would find a new home. Lila loaded up her van with all the dogs except Bralie. "What's the point of bringing Bralie?" she asked herself. "Who's going to take this dog?" After Lila left for the fair, her friend grabbed Bralie and followed. "You've got to give this dog a chance," the friend insisted.

Some two hours into the event, a young boy walked up, took a look at Bralie and told Lila that his friend once had a dog just like that but lost it. Lila dismissed the prospect of Bralie being the same dog as far too great a coincidence. An hour later, a burly man and his ten-year-old son approached, said a few words to Lila, and Bralie went crazy—jumping up and down, wagging her tail until it nearly fell off, howling, and whining a *I-haven't-seen-you-in-years* kind of whine. She recognized her master's voice. It was a joyous reunion—tears flowed and smiles shone brighter than the stars in Hollywood.

When things calmed down, the man explained that on July 4, frightened by fireworks, his blind dog jumped over a five-foot high fence and ran away. He looked for her at the local shelter (a different shelter than where she ended up), contacted authorities and posted signs throughout the neighborhood, but Bralie never materialized. One day a neighbor who knew the dog told the man that she had seen it lying dead in the road. Heartbroken, they stopped searching. Lila checked the facts to make sure Bralie was really their dog, and everything proved copacetic. When Lila later visited the father and son, she found Bralie "as happy as can be back in her own home. They belong together," she admits.

Lila advises that Bralie's nearly fatal adventure offers several important lessons. Pet owners should take extra precautions during the 4th of July and other times that may be stressful. If a pet is ever lost, there's always a chance that it could be found. Contact authorities. Personally visit shelters throughout the area. Run ads in newspapers. And "never give up hope."

Dallas

Advertising executives wanted a big, tough-looking dog for a light-hearted television commercial promoting the Dallas Stars professional hockey team. Hockey players are rugged; some fans are, too. The commercial needed to reinforce a tenacious image, so the talent agency called Desoto Feed and Animal Rescue in Desoto, Texas, in hopes of finding a bold, photogenic dog, perhaps a Doberman pinscher.

Unfortunately, Janie Blair, owner of the feed store that spends its profits saving the lives of abandoned and abused animals, was fresh out of Dobermans. She did, however, know of a 100-pound rottweiler named Dallas who just might score well with a television audience. At one point in time the three-year-old was even a bit "snappy," which was why a previous owner got rid of him. But with patience and kindness on the part of his new family, Dallas turned out "as sweet as can be." Janie convinced the talent scouts to give Dallas a shot. The morning Janie drove the fledgling pitch-dog to tape the commercial, he rested his head on her shoulder and licked her ear the entire way there.

Dallas had every reason to lavish his affections on Janie. She and her husband, Cotton, had taken him in as they had countless other unwanted animals who were deposited at the retail establishment/no-kill shelter over the years. Janie, a former member of corporate America, and Cotton, an active farmer, have rescued dogs, cats, rabbits, chickens, pigeons, doves, goats, calves, a goose and a malnourished horse. "A little bit of everything," says Janie. Many of the animals have been tied up on the store property at night under the cover of darkness, abandoned by their owners. One morning, Janie discovered in their parking lot a dog house with the dog chained to it; alongside sat his water and food bowls. "They (dog's owners) just washed their hands of him." Then there was the "kitten explosion," a single week when eighty meowing balls of fur showed up at their front door. Another time "we found five boxes on the doorstep with chickens, pigeons, rabbits and kittens stuffed inside," Janie remembers.

When the Blairs started the retail business, they didn't intend it to serve as an animal sanctuary. Things simply evolved that way. At first a few wounded or lost critters were dropped off. The Blairs took them in, nursed them back to health, and found them new homes. Eventually word of their kindness got out, and more and more animals were abandoned or surrendered. "We just never know what we are going to find," says Janie.

In addition to caring for the small animals at the store and the larger ones back at the farm, the Blairs designed a petting zoo that attracts kids of all ages. For fun now and then the proprietors shut the doors to the store and let some of the animals roam around inside.

"You'll see a goat run by or a dog chasing a cat," says Janie. "People come here out of curiosity to see what greets them." Janie also takes some of the animals to nursing homes as therapy for the residents and to schools for animal education seminars.

Many of the animals of Desoto Feed are adopted out to good homes, like Dallas was, but the sanctuary is an expensive undertaking. "It's a black hole for money," says Janie. Donations are always welcomed, as they are by virtually every shelter and rescue group throughout the country.

Oftentimes when Cotton finishes up work on the farm and stops by the store in the afternoon, he asks Janie: "Okay, what did you take in today?" Probably more than most people will in a lifetime.

As for Dallas, he performed beautifully for the cameras and feels quite comfortable with his newfound celebrity. Tough dogs make no bones about their talent.

Chelsea

Bud Mason spent much of his time alone after Donnabelle, his beloved wife, developed a serious illness and was hospitalized. Retired, with the children grown and out of the house, Bud wanted company. One day while he watched an afternoon newscast, a woman from Fort Wayne Animal Care & Control appeared on the television screen with a young tan-and-white mutt who needed a good home. "There was something about her," Bud thought to himself. "She was all by herself, and I was all by myself." Why not take a closer look?

He drove to the shelter, met the sociable puppy and decided then and there to adopt her. Bud and Chelsea hit it off right away. She behaved well, never jumped on the furniture, didn't mess in the house and, first and foremost, always wanted to be with people. "I couldn't have asked for a better companion," Bud says. "I thought the dog would be good company for my wife as well."

Donnabelle returned home after several months in the hospital, and Bud's prediction came true. Chelsea and Donnabelle grew very close. While the husband and wife enjoyed wonderful moments together in Indiana, their new pet seasoned the household with innocence and vigor.

"Older people have no idea how much company a dog can be," says Bud. "They need an animal more than younger people who have families and jobs."

As the years went by, Donnabelle's health deteriorated, but the bond between the woman and her dog grew ever stronger. Eventually confined to bed, Donnabelle need only look down at the floor to find Chelsea lying there beside her, wrapped in devotion. The dog would sit up, place her front paws on the bed and lean forward whenever she needed a reassuring pat on the head. Donnabelle always obliged. Sadly, Donnabelle passed away more than a decade after Chelsea came from the shelter. Bud firmly believes, however, that the dog's love and companionship "helped my wife live longer than she was intended to."

Although Donnabelle is no longer with them, her treasured memory lives on. Of course, Bud and Chelsea still have each other, and their daily routine keeps them busy. Each morning Bud goes into the bathroom and taps the dog's brush on the floor. Hearing the familiar cue, Chelsea runs in and sits quietly for a few minutes of grooming. They watch a little TV together and frequently go outside. "How many 84-year-olds will get out of the house four times a day and take a walk?" Bud asks proudly. In the afternoon, Bud often lies down for a nap; Chelsea hops up and snuggles beside him—the only time she's allowed on the furniture.

❦

Quest

Cruelty and neglect ravaged the Doberman pincher's body and soul as he stumbled through an opening in a fence and into a stranger's backyard one hot, humid morning. He saw an old mattress wasting away in the grass and decided to lie down on it and die. There was no reason to go on.

When animal control officers came to collect the emaciated four- or five-year-old, they discovered a dog who "took a wrong turn down Bad Owner Boulevard," as Kimberly Capella-Gowland of Gulf Coast Doberman Rescue in Long Beach, Mississippi, would say. Barely alive, "he was so weak, he couldn't even stand up." Open sores covered the outside of his body, the result of sarcoptic mange. Heartworms, hookworms and whipworms thrived inside. "He was a parasite on four paws," says Kimberly. Infection spread along his rear legs. Scars wrapped around his neck, telltale signs of a life spent fastened to a chain. An arrhythmia prevented his heart from beating properly. Fleas danced along the sections of his body worth inhabiting. The dog had more than enough reason to call it a day.

"A lot of people would have looked at him and given up," says Kimberly, whose group rescues, rehabilitates and places unwanted Dobermans in new homes. She had other ideas. Upon meeting the dog at a shelter where he was taken and awaited euthanasia, Kimberly looked into his "soulful eyes," bent down and wrapped her arms around the pitiful creature. "He needed a hug," she explains. He also needed lots of medical care, love and encouragement, which he received thanks to the rescuers who named him Quest. After months of recuperation, there was one more thing Quest needed: a good home.

Ann and Roy Hepler were more than happy to oblige. When they first met Quest, "he immediately took to us," says Ann. "There was something in his eyes" that assured the Heplers that Quest was the dog for them. They adopted him during football season—perfect timing, because Quest and Roy soon discovered they enjoy spending weekends together watching the pigskin move up and down the field on TV. Ann doesn't feel neglected, though; Quest always sets aside plenty of "love time" for mom. "He's a great dog," she says. He also loves to play with the Hepler's teenage son and Hailey, another Doberman the family adopted.

Quest demonstrated his devotion early one cold winter morning when Ann took him out for a walk. Going down the steps with Quest on a leash, Ann slipped on some ice and landed hard on her hip and elbow. She thought they were broken and at the same instant also feared that Quest would take off. Canine loyalty in this instance proved beyond question. "When he realized I was lying on the ground, he turned around, came back, laid next to me and put his head in my lap," Ann remembers. Quest had no intention of going anywhere before Roy arrived and Ann stood up safely. "Until I told him it was okay, he wasn't leaving me," she explains. As it turned out, there were no broken bones. Massive bruises emerged, but they were soothed by the realization of Quest's love and dedication.

He expressed his protective nature once again when Ann's friend, who had never met Quest, entered the house unexpectedly at 3 a.m. As the woman walked down a dark hallway to get a drink of water, the ninety-pound dog appeared like a vision in a bad dream and let out a "roar" that sounded like a lion on steroids. Roy and Ann rushed to the hallway to find their friend backed up against a wall. "He could have hurt her, but he didn't," says Ann. "He just stopped her from being able to get to us." An hour or so later the friend quit trembling and everyone retired for the night. Ann and Roy slid back into bed, and Quest assumed his normal position between the two of them. His current mattress is a tad more comfortable than the one he laid down on in that backyard so long, long ago.

Lady & Orson

They're in love, and they don't care who knows it. The couple met under less-than-ideal circumstances but managed—with a little help from their friends—to transform adversity into harmony simply by caring for one another.

Lady, a white shepherd mix and her beau, Orson, yellowish in color and of the same persuasion, were introduced in California. They lived together in the backyard of a doggy-dysfunctional home. The owner wasn't particularly interested in their well-being, providing little in terms of food, water or shelter. Oftentimes, the dogs wandered away in search of something to eat or drink. One day the hungry and thirsty pair hit pay dirt when they walked up to the doorstep of two animal lovers. The mother and daughter fed the dogs and then watched them amble off.

The next day they returned, then the next day, and the next. "He would wait for us to close the door, and then she would come out and eat first, and he would eat what remained; then they would go home," the daughter explained. Finally, the mother decided to follow the dogs, who led her to their fenced yard with a wide-open gate. She talked to the owner, who wasn't particularly cooperative. The following day, the dogs showed up again for something to eat. The pattern continued for months. A kindly animal control officer knew the pair roamed the streets, but understood that if he hauled them to the pound they would most likely be put to sleep.

Finally, the animal lovers had enough and asked the owner if they could take his dogs. With an expletive and a nod, he agreed. Unable to keep the dogs themselves, the mother and daughter faced the challenge of finding them a good home. A week later, Lady Luck blew in on a westward wind. There was an opening at Best Friends Animal Sanctuary in Utah, the largest no-kill animal haven in the country. The sanctuary agreed to take both dogs. The two women and the two dogs jumped in the car and headed east.

Best Friends accommodates up to 1,800 abandoned or abused dogs, cats and other animals in the scenic Angel Canyon, a few miles outside of Kanab. The animals receive medical care, shelter, plenty to eat and drink, and lots of attention beneath the blue western skies. "Most of them just need a few weeks of special care before they can go on to good, new homes," says Best Friends. "Others, who are older or sicker or have suffered extreme trauma, find a special home at the sanctuary for the rest of their lives." Best Friends' mission "is to help bring about a time when there are no more homeless pets, and when every cat or dog who's ever born can be guaranteed a good home with a loving family."

Into these surroundings, Lady and Orson settled. Unfortunately, Lady's health soon became an issue. Paralysis struck her back legs. At the in-house clinic, she barely ate or drank. She perked up when Orson came to visit, but that was it. "He watched intently while Lady was being examined and would kiss the vet staff when Lady confirmed with a look that she was not being hurt," explains Kristi Littrell.

"One morning when Lady couldn't even lift her head, we brought Orson over to see her," says Kristi. "The eight staff members who saw them together vowed they would work it out that the two dogs were never, ever separated again if Lady would just get better. As if completely understanding, Lady suddenly picked up her head with a spark in her eye and a thank-you in her heart. None of us had ever seen such a look of gratitude from two dogs before. Miraculously, she began to heal."

Over time, Lady's recovery progressed. She's still not a hundred percent but does well enough to go for daily walks with Orson, letting him know quite clearly that it is not okay for him to wander too far from her side. They share their own private living quarters in Best Friends' Dogtown, and when Lady goes to sleep in her doghouse, Orson lies next to it to make sure nothing goes wrong. They are inseparable and still very much in love. Sometimes they'll lie down together and cross paws. They like to touch, even after all this time.

Sugar

She was a mean dog. At least that was her reputation. The skinny boxer-pit bull mix roamed through the woods and fields of rural Virginia for at least a year, scavenging for food, worrying some of the locals and eluding authorities. On a hot summer day she gave birth to ten puppies and was forced to curtail her vagabond ways. That's when the game warden caught up with her.

He collared the four- or five-year-old mother and hauled the brindle and her brood off to the shelter. She was upset and let her captor know it. Believing that a stray mutt with a temper would most likely never be adopted, authorities agreed to let her finish nursing the puppies before taking the next step. In the interim, however, the shelter veterinarian discovered a gentle side to the new mom, who always made sure her puppies were fed and tended to before she took care of her own needs. The dog was so sweet, in fact, that the vet named her Sugar.

Maybe there was hope for this dog after all. The vet contacted Companion Animal Rescue Effort (CARE), a small Orange County organization that saves dogs and cats who have run out of chances. "Our main goal is to get

162

animals out of shelters and out of harm's way," explains CARE's Carole Santone who, together with her husband, Karl, rescues and finds homes for hundreds of dogs and cats a year.

When the puppies were ready to make it on their own, CARE took Sugar. One weekend soon afterwards she found herself with the Santones at a pet supply retailer that allows certain nonprofit organizations to showcase animals who are ready for adoption. At the same time, Suzanne Moe of Fredericksburg and her partner, Gaye, headed off to the store to buy some food for their cat, Mojo. It wasn't a pleasant outing, though; they were mourning the loss of their dog, Tootsie, who died three days earlier.

As they strolled toward the cat food aisle, Suzanne came upon Sugar. She stopped, took one look at the amiable dog, and was overcome by an inexplicable force. "I knew immediately that I was supposed to have her," says Suzanne. The chance meeting was so unexpected and the feeling so powerful, Suzanne was not quite sure what to think, but she knew they had to be together. "Sugar probably needed a home as much as I needed to heal. We would help each other," she thought. When Suzanne was about to finalize the adoption, she looked earnestly at Sugar and asked her opinion. The dog gently placed her paw onto Suzanne's hand. The handshake of sorts sealed the deal, providing the stray got along okay with the house cat.

Suzanne and Gaye set out for the store that day with no intention of adopting a dog, their grief still too profound. But destiny intervened and they returned home with the kitty kibble and a little Sugar. At first, the new home puzzled Sugar; she had probably never been inside one before. She was startled by the TV and the radio, even the staircase. But not by Mojo. When the dog and cat first met, they "looked at each other, touched noses, and that was that," Suzanne remembers.

Although Sugar seemed to be in pretty good shape, Suzanne took the dog to her own vet to be checked out. The exam showed that Sugar's left eye was totally blind and an x-ray found buckshot lodged in her left leg and side. She was such a playful, happy dog, no one suspected anything was wrong. The wounds were old, and nothing much could be done for them. Fortunately, they didn't hold her back one bit.

There was one ailment, however, that did need attention: separation anxiety. Now that she enjoyed loving companionship, Sugar didn't want to be left alone. The problem was serious enough for Suzanne to contact an animal communicator in hopes of finding out how to comfort the dog. The communicator suggested that Mojo stay in the house with Sugar when no one else was home. It worked. One other concern was that Sugar never barked. Amazingly, while Suzanne and the communicator were in the middle of discussing the situation, Sugar barked for the first time. Was it true communication with the animal or just coincidence? Some things can't be explained.

Over the last few years, Sugar has settled into her home and neighborhood quite nicely. "She's the most loving dog I've ever met," says Suzanne. Sugar feels fine, goes for walks and hangs out with Mojo and a new member of the family, a dog named Xak. Each pet has been rescued.

"People think that they can't make a difference, but they can," says Carole Santone. Just ask Sugar, that mean dog who used to live in the woods, or her puppies, who were all adopted by caring people.

‍❧

Lassie

They are a match made in heaven according to Felix Sunga, a trainer with the San Francisco SPCA Hearing Dog Program. He's referring to Bob Johnson, a retiree who suffers profound hearing loss, and his dog, Lassie, a collie-chow mix who languished in a California shelter before embarking on a new career as a hearing dog.

The moment they met it was clear that Bob and Lassie belonged together. After Bob enrolled in the SPCA program, Felix took five or six hearing dogs to the Johnson household to see if there would be a good match. Lassie instinctively gravitated to Bob as if their partnership was meant to be. Bob studied the other dogs, all excellent candidates, but Lassie made the greatest impression. Now they're inseparable. "Basically, she goes everywhere I go," says Bob.

"Hearing dogs can offer a practical alternative for many non-hearing people," according to the SF/SPCA. "The dogs are trained to respond to important sounds such as a knock at the door, doorbell, telephone or telecommunications device for the deaf, smoke alarm, alarm clock, timer device, or perhaps some other sound. Many deaf or hard-of-hearing people find that at some time they face the reality of missing important auditory signals—crucial, possibly life-saving warnings that most hearing people take for granted."

Bob believes Lassie's greatest contribution is her ability to help him interact with others. He explains that people who cannot hear sometimes feel isolated from the hearing world. "She helps me more than anything when we're out in public," he says. "She's not just helping me with sounds, but also with other people's perceptions. Her presence makes people more aware that I'm deaf, and I feel that I can better communicate with them."

Lassie was born to be a hearing dog, certainly not a ward of the state. She's smart, outgoing and loves to be around people. Generally, it takes a successful hearing dog candidate three to six months to learn the program. Lassie picked up the basics in two weeks. "She was an extremely quick study," says Felix. In fact, she's such a talented and helpful dog, Bob and Lassie spend one day a week at a rehabilitation center for people recovering from serious injuries and illness. Lassie helps the patients relax and interact with others and is especially successful with some of the victims who harbor anger and hostility due to their debilitation.

Despite the fact that she could give a canine television star a run for the money in terms of good deeds well done, Lassie does enjoy moments that are more suited to the comedy channel. One night at around eleven o'clock, she discovered a skunk in the backyard. The air around her cleared a few days later. Then there was the time Lassie, Bob and his wife, Winnie, were in church and

Lassie decided to harmonize during an especially moving hymn. She's talented, but there are limits.

The SF/SPCA notes that its hearing dog program, which gets most of its animals from shelters, "has resulted in a unique and exciting combination, offering assistance to deaf and hard-of-hearing individuals, while at the same time giving previously homeless animals a chance for useful lives of love and service."

The Johnsons would agree wholeheartedly. "We think we've got the greatest dog in the world," says Winnie. Sounds like Lassie came home to stay.

Jake

Jake was the skinniest dog the veterinarian ever saw. At thirty-six pounds, the balding Labrador retriever nearly starved before being rescued by the Humane Society of Cascade County in Great Falls, Montana. Open sores blemished what black coat remained on his skeletal frame, and he was covered with urine and feces when they found him imprisoned in a crate in his owner's backyard.

The smell was so bad and the dog so filthy, animal control officers left him in the container as they removed him from the premises that spring day and carted him off to the vet's office. When they opened the crate door and let him out, Jake moved slowly and cautiously, like an old man whose joints stiffened from disuse. But his inner nature remained intact. "As bad a shape as he was in, he could still give me a tail wiggle," explains the shelter's Susan Dendy.

Being allowed to stand up, move around and sniff fresh air were a most welcome reprieve for Jake. A long, hot bath scrubbed clean the memories of his filthy existence, and the soothing hand of a concerned veterinarian treated his wounds. Cool, refreshing water and wholesome food nourished his young body. After a few days of medical care, Jake headed off to the shelter in hopes of finding a new home.

The humane society lavished Jake with lots of TLC. He soon began to put on weight and enjoy his newfound freedom. "He has the biggest heart of any dog I have ever seen," says Susan. "It never broke his spirit." But he still needed a home.

Sometimes, things just work out well. Jake's original owner served in the military, and the serviceman's supervisor heard about the ordeal. The supervisor felt badly and decided to foster Jake until a permanent home could be found. That didn't take very long though, because the foster parent and his family quickly fell in love with the happy Lab, and they adopted him themselves, exactly one month after Jake first smelled the scent of freedom.

"Nowadays Jake has a full agenda with obedience and agility training, but he still finds time to drop in and see me from time to time," explains Susan. "As for the original owner, well, the Air Force takes care of its own, and he got what he deserved." Part of his punishment included working at the shelter.

Butch

(Florida)

A few months after Carol Hall saved Butch, the beagle-basset hound mix grew lethargic and began falling to the floor and stiffening. Alarmed by the episodes and knowing full well that young beagles are generally energetic and sure-footed, Carol contacted a heart specialist, who diagnosed the two-year-old with a cardiac problem known as sinus block. His heart beat just twelve times per minute. If Butch were to have any chance at a normal life, he would need a pacemaker.

The dog was jolly and very overweight when Carol first took him into her home, which also serves as Ziggy Beagle Rescue. His previous owner booted him after their relationship soured, perhaps because Butch suffered from separation anxiety and soothed his loneliness by mischief-making when left by himself. The behavior was unacceptable to his master, so he kept the dog crated most of the time. Young beagles are designed to run and chase scents, not languish in cages.

Carol started the small rescue organization several years earlier in Palm Bay, Florida, and named it after her first beagle, who died of cancer. The mission is to save unwanted beagles, rehabilitate them if necessary, and then find permanent, loving homes. Some of her guests are strays, others come from shelters or private homes. A few of Ziggy's beagles have gone to work for the U.S. Department of Agriculture, detecting fruits, vegetables and meat illegally smuggled into the country through airports.

With her husband ill, Carol handles the bulk of the work herself but also has the assistance of outside foster homes that help take care of some of the dogs until they are adopted. "I am constantly providing food, bathing dogs, cleaning ears and clipping toenails," explains Carol. She also must find ways to pay for their care.

Fortunately for Butch, St. Jude's Hospital in Memphis, Tennessee, donated a pacemaker. A cardiologist in Gainesville, Florida, performed the surgery, and Butch "came through the operation with flying colors." The device was set at 100 beats per minute, a rhythm better suited to the active doggy lifestyle.

Butch returned to Ziggy's to recuperate and soon was "very close to being a normal dog." Then the seizures returned. There were more tests, and this time they found that Butch had epilepsy. Medication was prescribed to keep it in check. A bad heart, epilepsy and hip dysplasia that had been discovered earlier. What else could go wrong with this poor dog with the sad beagle eyes?

Over the course of the next several years, Butch came down with a bum thyroid, high blood pressure and diabetes insipidus. But the patient never complains;

dogs rarely do. He enjoys life every day, plays with his friends and "acts like a normal dog is supposed to act," says Carol. "He's a very loving dog."

Very expensive, too. His medical bills climbed to at least $10,000, but Carol never thought twice about affording him the necessary care. She's grown so fond of Butch that he's no longer up for adoption. This one's a keeper, pacemaker and all.

∾⊶⊷∾

Fred & Pepper

Fred and Pepper grew old together in the Bronx, New York, snoozing at leisure, sharing a bite at mealtime, and taking those welcomed walks when nature called. Pepper, a female border collie mix, suffered seizures on occasion, and a malignant tumor offered cause for concern, but she seemed to be getting along fairly well. Fred enjoyed relatively good health, just the normal aches and pains brought on by age. All in all, there was nothing much to complain about, until one cold day their peaceful lives went up in smoke.

The building in which they lived caught fire and, abruptly, Pepper and Fred found themselves homeless. With no place else to go, their owner surrendered the two dogs to a shelter. Considering their age, both ten or eleven, and Pepper's questionable health, their future appeared as dark as ash. "They (shelter officials) called us and asked if we would take them, because they knew they had to stay together, and older dogs are not easy to adopt," explains Marcello Forte, executive director of Animal Haven, a no-kill shelter in Queens. "We took them immediately. They would almost certainly have been put down if we hadn't."

Animal Haven regarded Fred and Pepper as a couple who should spend the remainder of their days together. The rescuers showed the dogs at adoption events and posted photos on the Internet, but no one seemed interested. Several months later a Brooklyn couple with a teenage boy and a fenced-in backyard spotted the animals on a website. "Their faces looked so cute," the family agreed. A meeting was scheduled, and before long, Pepper and Fred headed to a new home in a neighboring borough.

The welcoming committee included the family's two cats, Riley and Emma. Riley greeted the newcomers warmly; Emma hissed her regards. Once the fur settled, the animals established their own boundaries and agreed to a detente. Fred and Pepper adjusted to their new surroundings in a New York minute, endeared themselves to the family, and made friends with the neighborhood children. Pepper's health stabilized over time, and now and then she displays a surprising degree of energy, enough to prompt her to dance on hind legs when a suitable human partner steps forward. The cocker spaniel-mix finds pleasure resting his tired bones on the couch next to a warm body and petting fingers. He especially likes to roll over for a soothing belly-rub.

Now that the smoke has cleared for Fred and Pepper, life is back to normal. Of course, there have been changes, big ones, but the two old companions still have each other. They are safe and loved and about ready for a nap.

Dallie

She found a home and then lost it, found a different home and then lost it, found yet another home and then lost it, too. Dallie's family history is sketchy at best, but it's fairly certain the friendly dalmatian with the engaging "smarl" (a cross between a smile and a snarl) now lives in her fifth household with the O'Sullivan family in the State of Washington, and she's finally home to stay.

Dallie is a by-product of Hollywood. Popular dalmatian movies produced some years ago inspired enthusiastic would-be dog owners to scurry to pet stores and breeders to bring home a darling little puppy of their own. To the surprise of far too many of these people, puppies require constant work and eventually grow to be adults—still great animals, but not quite so darling. The result: countless dalmatians abandoned or surrendered to shelters throughout the country. Dallie is one of the lucky ones; she survived.

Alison O'Sullivan, who together with her husband rescue dogs through their organization, Coonhound Opportunities Organization Northwest, saw Dallie on the website, Petfinder.com. She kept her eye out for a dalmatian to adopt as a companion for her other dalmatian.

They had two coonhounds as well, but Alison believed another dalmatian would be a better playmate. Scrolling down the computer screen one day, Dallie's face stopped Alison in her tracks. "Her Petfinder picture is what did it," Alison admits. "I was looking for a dalmatian and didn't want to purchase one from a store; I wanted a rescue."

Coincidentally, Dallie lived nearby with a couple who was about to have a baby and decided dogs no longer fit in the picture. When Alison first met the sociable animal, "Dallie put her arms around my waist and smarled at me." Hugs are hard to resist. The five-year-old dog wearing a short white coat spattered with black spots was about to relocate.

Dallie now has a wonderful life. "She is energetic and involved," says Alison. "She's not going to lay in a corner and let the world pass her by." Dallie and her mates go on hikes, play fetch, ride around, do all kinds of things. "They go everywhere with me," says Alison. What about the emotional trauma associated with bouncing from home to home? Alison believes it takes a toll on a dog. "Animals are attached; people don't realize that when they dump their animals," she says. Dallie can be moody and insecure at times, in all likelihood the result of earlier instability. Her future, however, is built on a solid foundation. "I often tell her this is the last home she's going to have," says Alison.

Eat your heart out, Cruella.

⸎

Red

And it came to pass: a blessed event that claimed more than its share of saintly mystique. On a star-filled night just before Saint Valentine's Day a huge Saint Bernard-catahoula mix miraculously entered through locked gates and laid down to rest inside an isolation run at the Saint Tammany Humane Society in Covington, Louisiana. (Another theory holds that someone managed to get inside and abandoned her there.) Either way, she was a sweetheart. At least a canine suitor thought so.

The big, beautiful dog gave birth in the shelter on Valentine's Day to Zoe, Shasta, Avalon, Summer, Autumn, Winter, Red, Blizzard, Forest and Hurricane. The adorable puppies grew strong and healthy and kept the Saint Tammany staff entertained as well as busy. An unexpected animal arriving at a filled shelter is one thing, but when she delivers ten others, that becomes burdensome. Nonetheless, the staff carried on and eventually found homes for the mother and all of her children, except for Zoe, who still longs for a "forever home with lots of unconditional love."

As the puppies awaited adoption, the staff believed Red would be the hardest to place. He was the biggest of the litter, quite gangly and a bit headstrong. "But with his deep, glowing chestnut coat and one blue eye and one brown, who could resist?" asks Saint Tammany's Deborah Hatch. Red loved to play whenever the opportunity arose; his long legs, growing body and bushy tail flopped here and there as the happy-go-lucky youngster discovered the wonders of puppy-hood. The staff worked on obedience skills with Red, and it didn't take him too long to catch on. Surely, someone would adopt this "magnificent looking dog."

One day a veterinarian who provided medical services to the shelter saw Red sitting all alone at the end of his run. He and his wife, also a vet, already had cats, another dog and several horses, but the doctor took an interest in Red all the same. "The more he got to know him, the more he liked him," recalls Deborah. Eventually, the veterinarians decided to adopt the happy, clumsy mutt with the wonderful personality. Although the shelter staff was overjoyed that Red found such a great home, "we cried when he went," admits Deborah.

Not long afterward, the vets and their pets packed up and moved to Ohio. Red, who now weighs in at 110 pounds, runs and plays with his companions on several acres of land and enjoys the security of a loving home, not to mention great healthcare benefits.

A wise man might wonder what would have become of Red, his siblings, his mother and all of the other abandoned animals were it not for the saints who look out for them.

⤳⤳⤳

Rocky

But for the kindness of strangers, Rocky's young life would have come to a screeching halt one cold, rainy night in March. The bull mastiff puppy and a friend were scampering through the darkness like two carefree children, enjoying the liberating adventure of dogs on the loose, until, out of nowhere, a car barreled down the road and struck Rocky head-on. As he crumbled to the pavement, Rocky saw his friend dash away, perhaps slightly injured, but not nearly as badly as he.

The shocked six-month-old lay in the middle of the road howling in pain for what seemed like an eternity while passersby slowed to take a look and then sped up and kept on going. A woman working in a nearby grocery store heard the dog's cries and called authorities for help. No one came. She called another agency. Still no response. As Rocky moaned in agony, she grabbed a phone book and hurriedly dialed other numbers hoping to find someone who could lend assistance. Finally, a woman who happened to be driving by stopped. With help, she lifted the sixty-pound dog into her car and hastened to a veterinary clinic.

Elia Ginn of Animal Rescue Families in Bremerton, Washington, was one of the people contacted by the woman from the grocery store. Before Elia could respond from her home twenty-five miles away, Rocky was already on his way to the clinic. Concerned, Elia called the veterinarian later on to check the dog's condition. The prognosis looked grim. The automobile shattered Rocky's left, front shoulder, and his right, front leg suffered severe injury. Elia told the vet to administer pain medication and her group would pick up the tab. "We assumed the responsibility," says Elia.

She went to visit Rocky the following morning. "He was a gorgeous dog with a beautiful face," Elia remembers. "The tail started wagging the minute you went into the hospital room." Rocky desperately needed surgery, but first an effort had to be made to find his owner. A situation like this can get a bit sticky. Rocky wore no identifying tags, but performing surgery before notifying the owner and establishing who would cover the costs left some doubts as to the next move.

Police and animal control officials were notified and fliers distributed near the scene of the accident. Several days later, the owner turned up but said he couldn't afford the medical treatment. Although her small rescue group didn't have the resources to pay for the surgery and follow-up care either, Elia agreed to do so, and the owner allowed the rescuers to assume permanent responsibility for the dog.

Doctors operated on Rocky for five and a half hours in an effort to piece together the shoulder and repair the other leg. The dog remained in the clinic for two months and, sadly, lost the right leg anyway. Recovery continued for many months thereafter in a foster home. Rocky had to learn to get along on three legs. To make matters worse, when he walked all his forward weight rested heavily on the damaged and painful left front shoulder. He persevered, nonetheless.

"Finally, we decided he was ready for adoption," says Elia. A couple who owned and loved a three-legged dog for twelve years before it died heard about Rocky and asked to adopt him. They passed muster, and Rocky now enjoys a comfortable and happy life, together with another dog and a cat.

For the rescue group, though, there was a $6000 medical bill to cover. Once again, a stranger stepped up. A man who barely had enough money to handle his own bills heard about Rocky and paid most of the veterinary costs. "A lot of people put their hearts into this little guy," says Elia. Rocky has a knack for bringing out the best in human nature.

Moses

The elderly Arizona couple faced a difficult reality: the time had come to enter a special care facility, but their beloved, nearly twelve-year-old Maltese could not join them. No pets allowed. Senior citizens confront this dilemma on a regular basis. They agonize over the prospect of their faithful companions suddenly ending up alone at the pound facing imminent death. Sometimes, a family member or friend will take the pet, although that's not always possible. Such was the case with Moses the ultimate lap dog, a tiny, white purebred whose tongue constantly hung out the side of his mouth, making him look like a cartoon character.

Desperate to do all they could to save Moses, the couple contacted a rescue group that agreed to help him find a new home. The rescuers, in turn, brought him and his little basket lined with a soft pad to Sun Cities Animal Rescue in Glendale, a no-kill shelter that takes in more than its share of animals stuck in this predicament. "He was adorable," remembers Sara Martinez of Sun Cities. "Funny, but adorable." Because of his age and the hanging tongue (a cosmetic problem believed to have been caused as a result of several permanent teeth failing to grow in), the shelter feared it would be difficult to place

Moses. Small young dogs are usually adopted quickly at Sun Cities; for an older dog with a silly grin, finding a home could be more difficult than parting the Red Sea.

Sara took to Moses right away and decided to foster him until his adoption day finally arrived. On the job, he sat in Sara's lap as she worked the front desk at the shelter. He went home with her in the evening and followed her every move until she sat down, at which point Moses hopped onto Sara's lap and snuggled up in the position he loved best. "He was the biggest lap dog I ever saw," says Sara. At night, Moses climbed into his little basket and slept by the foot of Sara's bed.

"Moses was absolutely content as long as he was near me," explains Sara. Although he always appeared happy, there had to be some degree of anxiety simmering deep within the Moses psyche. He once lived a comfortable lap-dog life with two people who loved him very much. Then all of a sudden they, and his home, were gone. After a confusing couple of days, he moved in with someone else who cared deeply, but what would happen next? Moses never wanted to put any distance between himself and Sara, perchance she might go missing, too. "If I was gone, he got lonely," says Sara. Separation is difficult for animals as well as people. It can be tragic to give up a pet when age dictates circumstance.

Fortunately for some Sun Cities animals, there are other senior citizens living in the area who own their own homes, sans pet restrictions, and welcome four-pawed companionship. The shelter staff figured that sooner or later a retired woman who wanted a gentle, friendly lap dog would browse around and find the Moses' charm irresistible. To their surprise and delight, a middle-aged man who makes a habit of saving animals first saw Moses outside a pet store on an adoption day and set his sights on the little critter. A few days later, he came to the shelter to learn more. Up to his old tricks, Moses made himself comfortable in the man's lap. The guy "fell in love immediately," says Sara.

Moses' days of uncertainty are over. He's safe, happy and anxious no more, living with the man and his band of other animals in the country. He sleeps in his little basket at night and still continues to pester until he lands on a warm lap. Sara misses the little guy but recognizes a positive outcome when she sees it. "I was sad (to see him go) but I knew he had a good, permanent home," she affirms. "It put my heart at ease."

ᐧᗕᑐᗢ

Bandit

One of the great things that endears dogs to those who love them is their ability to ignore their troubles and move forward. Bandit exemplifies the complaining-gets-you-nowhere/positive-performance-is-what-really-matters attitude to which most dogs subscribe.

The Australian shepherd mix was only three months old when he was surrendered to the Kentucky Humane Society in Louisville. He arrived with chewing gum and candy stuck to the flap of his ear like badges of mistreatment. More critically, an elastic band encircled his left, front leg. It had been there for far too long, choking off the blood supply and cutting through muscle and tissue all the way to the bone. His little tendons were destroyed, infection had set in, and the leg required amputation at the shoulder.

"He was in a pathetic state, but he had a personality that stole everyone's hearts and markings that make him look like he is wearing a mask. From then on, he was called Bandit," explains the humane society's Tara Blandford.

After the surgery and an overnight stay in the clinic, Bandit went home to recuperate with Darren Bradshaw, the humane society's weekend veterinary technician. Darren took care of the puppy's medical needs and agreed to foster the amputee until a permanent home could be found. That didn't take long. Bandit hit it off so well with Darren's eight-year-old beagle mix, Mick, Darren decided to adopt the dog himself.

Rehabilitation progressed swiftly. It would take more than an amputation to keep this working dog down for too long. In a few weeks, Bandit was up and walking. Soon he was running around and challenging Mick to the age-old canine pastime, tug-of-war. Now that Bandit is fully recovered, the dogs have a ball together, wrestling, playing, and enjoying each other's companionship. "Bandit is just as active as other dogs," says Darren. "He doesn't seem to miss the leg at all."

Because he was abused at such an early age, "you'd think that he would be timid," suggests Darren. He's not, not even close. When he walks through downtown Louisville, Bandit never misses a chance to say hello to strangers. He's also no stranger to colleagues at the advertising agency where Darren works full-time. In fact, Bandit goes to the office so often, he has his own nameplate on a door. Advertising is a tough business that relies on top performers. Bandit will do well.

∾⚓∿

Rosco

He stands tall and proud, yet the handsome two-year-old boxer named Rosco is just a big baby at heart. Friendly and spirited, with a level of energy rivaling that battery-peddling bunny on TV commercials, he epitomizes the breed. With a little luck—maybe a lot of luck—his exuberance will live on for years to come.

Rosco's fortunes have risen and fallen like those of a gambler on a roll. He left home one day only to discover that no one wanted him to return. Eventually picked up as a stray, he spent time in a Wyoming shelter until Shelley Cumella of Black Hills Boxer Rescue in Rapid City, South Dakota, drove 250 miles to arrange for his release and offer the outcast a new shot at life.

His future brightened . . . briefly. When Shelley brought Rosco to the veterinarian for an examination, the doctor found several bad teeth, a missing toe and a marble-sized lump beneath his light brown coat The lump turned out to be malignant, surprising everyone because of his age. The cancerous growth was removed, and Shelley and another rescuer brought Rosco to their homes to foster him and decide whether, given his condition, he should be considered for adoption. There was already a family interested, but the newly detected health concern might change their minds.

At his foster homes, Rosco demonstrated why his original owner made no effort to take him back. At first he jumped around and climbed on counters, tables, furniture and any other place that looked inviting. "He obviously had no clue how to behave in a home," says Shelley. He didn't do too well in a barn, either, where he tried boxing several horses. "Boxers are very goofy, mischievous dogs," Shelley admits. After a few weeks of training, though, Rosco learned proper behavior, settled down and changed into a welcomed house guest. "He's truly one of the sweetest dogs we've ever had come through our program," says Shelley. "If people would spend a little bit of time, they could make any dog into a perfect pet."

The family adopted Rosco despite his questionable health. Unfortunately, a few weeks later, another tumor surfaced. During the subsequent operation, the surgeon removed six more lumps, all malignant, grade two, mast cell tumors. The likelihood of the cancer returning remains high. Nonetheless, the family has no intention of sending Rosco back. "They absolutely love this dog and will keep him for as much time as he has left," says Shelley, adding that it is unusual to come across people who are this kind. Rosco shares his new home with a one-eyed fish and a turtle with half a shell. He's especially close to a young boy in the family who was seriously injured by a car. "The boy feels really connected to Rosco," says Shelley.

People should consider the quality of the time they spend with a special needs pet, not the length of time, according to Shelley. It's a safe bet that Rosco will enjoy the remainder of his days, however many there may be, in a devoted, caring environment. Good luck, Rosco.

৶৩৶৶

Scrappie

Nick met Scrappie after the affectionate rottweiler-mix bounced from one home to another, finally landing in a shelter where he was branded "unadoptable." Some of Nick's friends at the MacLaren Correctional Facility in Woodburn, Oregon, experienced similar displacement, moving in and out of foster homes, trapped in a cycle of uncertainty. Fortuitously, the incarcerated youths provided Scrappie one last chance to live.

As euthanasia waited silently around the corner from Scrappie's pen, a Project Pooch manager decided to pay him a visit. Project Pooch is a nonprofit organization that matches unwanted dogs with young people at MacLaren who obedience train the animals and prepare them for adoption as family pets. It stands to reason that some abandoned and abused youngsters empathize with animals who suffer similar fates.

The program offers "a new leash on life to both the rescued dogs and the juvenile offenders," according to Project Pooch. "For some, this is their first experience of unconditional love." Students train the dogs daily, practicing positive reinforcement and behavior modification. "They learn that praise works, not punishment," says

Joan Dalton, founder of Project Pooch. As the students manage their dogs, they learn how to manage their own behavior.

Scrappie appeared to be a good Project Pooch candidate. Friendly, outgoing and housebroken, the energetic young dog's primary misconduct involved his desire to escape from time to time, hopping over a fence for an afternoon jaunt or a round of cat-chasing. Thanks to Project Pooch, Scrappie escaped a death sentence. He joined the organization's unique program and teamed up with Nick, an experienced student trainer. The intelligent dog learned quickly as a result of Nick's patience and dedication. Within three months, armed with a new set of manners, Scrappie was ready to move on.

A family with a horse farm in southern Oregon took an interest in Scrappie. As Joan drove the dog to his potentially permanent home, she thought to herself: "The test is going to be how Scrappie gets along with horses." She found out when they arrived. Scrappie scouted out the place before walking up to one of the horses for a get acquainted sniff. The horse lowered its head as if greeting an old friend, and then the two animals rubbed noses. "I was just in awe," says Joan. "I couldn't have asked for anything better." Family members were impressed as well and suggested that Scrappie spend the night as a trial before making a final commitment. The next morning Project Pooch received a call asking if Scrappie could stay.

Scrappie is a prime example of why people who adopt pets—only to return them when things don't work out just right—probably shouldn't adopt them in the first place. An animal who is repeatedly surrendered is deemed "unadoptable," which usually translates to euthanasia. "When you get a pet, it is a lifetime commitment," says Joan.

❧

Shredder & Sissy

Shredder ran into the bedroom in the middle of the night and started licking Michael George's face. Half asleep and remembering that he needed to get up for church in a few hours, Michael told the black lab to go lie down. The dog reluctantly obeyed. As Michael started to drift off, Sissy, the George's dalmatian, bounded into the room and landed on top of his stomach. That got Michael's attention and, as he bolted straight up, so did the dreadful smell of smoke. He immediately yelled to his wife, Rita, who was sleeping in another bedroom with their five-year-old grandson, Broderick: "The house is on fire. Get out."

Rita wasted no time. She picked up her grandson, tucked him under her arm "like a football," and used her other hand to feel her way through the blackened night, desperately trying to find the front door. By then, thick, acrid smoke filled the entire house, and flames leapt through the walls like ghosts dancing in a nightmare. After what must have seemed like an eternity, the grandmother and her grandson made it to safety. "I got out and immediately took Broderick to our next-door neighbor," Rita remembers. Then she ran back to look for Michael and her two dogs.

Rita stood nervously outside the flaming house as her husband picked up the dalmatian and pushed her through the bedroom window. Rita tugged on Sissy's paws and managed to pull her out. Michael climbed through the window behind the dog, as their home of thirty years burned away. At least they made it out—everyone that is, except for Shredder. The thirteen-year-old lab remained inside, perhaps still obeying the command to lie down until it became too late to get back up. "Shredder was still inside in the fire," says Rita. "We thought he was dead."

Both dogs were beloved family pets. Shredder started life as a stray and came to the Georges as a puppy. Sissy was adopted from the Nebraska Humane Society years later. They were great companions—Shredder, friendly bold and always on guard, while Sissy's reserved personality enhanced her gentle nature. As firemen rushed to the scene, it appeared the dogs' relationship would end in tragedy.

However, amid the turmoil and devastation of that cold December night in Omaha, a flicker of good fortune appeared in the arms of a firefighter. Shredder was alive. He suffered from smoke inhalation but was not burned. After several months, he recovered fully.

Authorities determined that an overloaded circuit caused the fire. The house was totally destroyed, but no one died, thanks in large part to Shredder and Sissy. In recognition of their heroism, the dogs received a special award from the Nebraska Kennel Club. "We're so happy to have them," says Rita. "They're really good dogs."

❧

Buddy

It saved his life. A small identification tag that hung from Buddy's collar enabled the pit bull-shar-pei mix to return safely from a transcendent journey that most certainly would have ended in death.

For a young dog, Buddy experienced his share of hard times. His first family surrendered him to the Hillside SPCA in Pottsville, Pennsylvania, because they were moving and Buddy wasn't allowed to come. This happens frequently within the canine community.

Nonetheless, the "happy-go-lucky" Buddy recovered from his loss and got along well with everyone at the shelter, humans as well as animals. "He was real easy to deal with . . . an all-around good dog," says the SPCA's Tricia Moyer. Buddy stayed at the no-kill shelter for approximately one month, until he found a new home. As expected, he hit it off with his new family, including their other dog. It appeared Buddy had bounced back.

A few months later, the Hillside SPCA received a phone call from a shelter in Nebraska saying they had Buddy and the youthful, good-natured dog would be put to sleep in one week if Hillside didn't retrieve him. The Nebraska shelter does not adopt out pit bulls, so Buddy had only one chance to live. The identification tag affixed to his collar bought him that chance. "We can't stress it enough that animals have to be ID-ed," says Tricia. "Without an ID tag, he would have been just another stray dog."

How did Buddy get from Pennsylvania to Nebraska that summer? Evidently, his family moved there (Buddy doesn't do well with moves), although the SPCA was never able to reach them to confirm. How did he wind up in the Nebraska shelter? Only Buddy knows for sure.

At least Buddy was safe, for the time being. Hillside needed to act quickly, though, to save his life. They hooked up with a rescuer in Nebraska who offered assistance. She took Buddy to a no-kill shelter and helped arrange for his transportation back to Pennsylvania. Thanks to the Internet, they were able to contact volunteers who drove Buddy along various legs of the journey. An animal-loving Colorado couple who happened to read the appeal on the Internet chauffeured Buddy the bulk of the way, putting him up in some nice hotels en route. "People always need help transporting animals," says Tricia. "The Internet was his godsend."

When he arrived back in Pottsville, everyone greeted the well-traveled mutt with warm affection and relief. Buddy's excellent, but nearly fatal, adventure earned a spot on a television news program, which prompted several people to call the shelter and express interest in giving him a home. A large family (one that is not moving anywhere soon) adopted the "travelin' man," and now Buddy lives in a nice house with lots of people to entertain and a cat to bother. "We all love him," his "forever" family told the SPCA. "Thank you for what you do."

About the Author

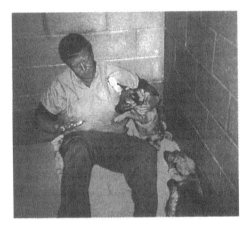

Dog lover Steve Swanbeck started writing about abandoned and abused animals in the early 1980s, during his days as a newspaper editor. The stories helped many unwanted dogs and cats find new homes, including a little, black dog who was hit by a car in New York City and lay injured at the side of the road for three days until a Good Samaritan from New Jersey stopped and carried him to safety. The dog went on to live a long and happy life. The author's last book recorded the history of Seeing Eye dogs, extraordinary animals who help thousands of people who are blind or visually impaired achieve greater independence. Steve (shown volunteering at Best Friends Animal Sanctuary in Utah) will donate a portion of his proceeds from *Disposable Dogs* to help homeless animals.